LEGACY
of a
Pack Rat

LEGACY
of a
Pack Rat

Ruth Bell Graham

Illustrated by
Floyd E. Hosmer

OLIVER
NELSON

A Division of Thomas Nelson Publishers
Nashville

Published in Nashville, Tennessee, by Oliver-Nelson Books, a division of Thomas Nelson, Inc., Publishers, and distributed in Canada by Lawson Falle, Ltd., Cambridge, Ontario.

Unless otherwise noted, Scripture quotations are from The King James Version of the Holy Bible or are paraphrases. Other Scripture quotations, as noted, are from the Revised Standard Version of the Bible, copyrighted 1946, 1952, © 1971, 1973; *The New English Bible*, © the Delegates of the Oxford University Press 1961, 1970, reprinted by permission; and *The Bible: A New Translation*, copyrighted 1922, 1924, 1925, 1926, 1935, by Harper and Brothers, © 1950, 1952, 1953, 1954 by James A. R. Moffatt.

Every effort has been made to contact the owners or owners' agents of copyrighted material for permission to use their material. If copyrighted material has been included without the correct copyright notice or without permission, due to error or failure to locate owners/agents or otherwise, we apologize for the error or omission and ask that the owner or owner's agent contact Oliver-Nelson and supply appropriate information. Correct information will be included in any reprinting.

37—AGAINST ALL ODDS: Newspaper article reprinted courtesy of the *Baptist Record*, Jackson, Mississippi.
53—GOD BLESS AND FORTIFY THEM: Poem, "For All People," from *Halfway Up the Sky* by Jane Merchant. Copyright © 1985 by Elizabeth Merchant. Used by permission of Abingdon Press.
56—SMALL PRAYERS: Poem, "And then a little laughing prayer," from *Rose from Brier* by Amy Carmichael, copyright 1933 Dohnavur Fellowship (London: S.P.C.K.; Ft. Washington, PA: Christian Literature Crusade). Used by permission.

"This special Billy Graham Evangelistic Association edition is published with permission of the original publisher, Oliver-Nelson Books, a division of Thomas Nelson, Inc., Publishers, Nashville, Tennessee.

Printed in the United States.

Jacket: Koeschel/Peterson Design
Interior Mouse Illustrations: Floyd E. Hosmer
Interior Design: Harriette Bateman
Typesetting: ProtoType Graphics, Inc.

Library of Congress Cataloging-in-Publication Data

Graham, Ruth Bell.
    Legacy of a pack rat / Ruth Bell Graham.
       p.   cm.
    ISBN 0-8407-9085-6 CB: ISBN 0-8407-9577-7 PB
    I. Title.
PS3557.R222L4   1989
818'.5409—dc19   88-32466
                                                     CIP

For you.

·······CONTENTS

········Three Cheers!

Three cheers for all who helped get this little legacy collected and presentable . . .

Evelyn Freeland, who typed and retyped and retyped with never a groan or sigh—thank you!

Maury Scobee, who, along with Evelyn and Victor Oliver, turned both dining room and kitchen in our house into an office-editorial room until we had carefully gone through each chapter. And made the work fun!

Victor Oliver, who urged me to write this, helped sort out old columns and poems, and then waited patiently until I was able to set aside time to sort through the artic of my mind, journals, letters, and such.

Lila Empson of Oliver-Nelson, who was in charge of the cleanup operations like spelling, punctuation, credits, typos, and such.

Andy Andrews, our neighbor, who caught the Pack Rat in her attic for the back cover.

Steve Griffith, who has worked tirelessly, smoothing the way.

Floyd Hosmer, whose exquisite etchings caught my fancy long before I knew anything about him, and who has designed the rat, trying to make her more appealing, than appalling!

And for all who have enriched my life by their stories and quotations by just being themselves. Some so disguised they would never recognize themselves. Others quoted with permission. Some just quoted.

Last but not least, there's Bill, my husband, who when I couldn't see the trees for the woods (or is it the other way around?) cheered me along!

This book was given to Samaritan's Purse-World Medical Mission before I actually started it. And if the publishers break even and there is anything left over, it all goes to God's work in this unique ministry.

1 · · · · · · By Way of Introduction

"You need to get a bulldozer to clean out your attic," Bill exclaimed one day. "All that junk—just clean it out and burn it. You'll never use it. And what will the family do with it after you're gone?"

"Get a bulldozer and clean it out," I replied.

And so it went. For years. And the wonderful old attic continued to accept contributions graciously, endlessly, never complaining.

A trunk going back to my childhood in China . . . Newspaper clippings of the fall of Shanghai to the Japanese in 1937 . . . High school in Korea, old love letters from Bill, boxes of photographs . . . An old Roman earthenware bowl dug up from the Thames River . . . A box of arrowheads and spearheads from Australia . . . Crutches to fit any height . . . Christmas ornaments . . . My old wedding dress (the veil was used to trim four bassinets; when Ned, the fifth, arrived he had to make do with a cradle) . . . Enough old luggage to start a used luggage shop . . .

A veritable treasure trove of disorganized surprises.

"When are you going to clear out the attic—all that old stuff you save? You'll never use it. The children won't know what to do with it—"

And so it has gone. Year after year.

One night Bill sat in the kitchen-den, ignoring the TV evening news, unthinkable for him. He was buried in a pile of notebook papers.

"Just look at these!" he exclaimed. "The best stuff I've ever come across in all these years since Bible school . . ."

"What are they?" I asked.

"My old Bible school notes."

"Where did you happen to get them?"

"At the Graham Center. They kept originals, but they gave me these photocopies."

I switched off the TV.

"And where did they happen to get that old notebook?" I asked.

Bill looked blank.

"Would you believe the attic?"

The next day Bill was talking on the phone telling a friend about his recent find. The friend must have asked him the same question I did, "Where had the archivist discovered the notebook?"

"Oh," Bill replied casually, "it was found in Ruth's attic."

Three cheers for Pack Rats!

Our minds are like storage attics. The experts tell us they save everything we ever heard, saw, or experienced; stored away there somewhere.

We may not be able to find it, but it's there.

Some of the bits and pieces stored away in my memory I've jotted down to enjoy or think about when I can't sleep or am too tired to stir around much, or simply have the need to reflect on times past, friends, funny events, how the Lord's goodness and mercy have followed me all the days of my life.

Here and there may surface something lost long ago and, I thought, forever.

2·····Missing Husband

When I answered the knock at the front door, the man standing there identified himself as a member of the F.B.I.

"I don't want to alarm you," he said, "but I must warn you there has been a threat on your husband's life and we felt it serious enough to warn you to take every precaution."

I thanked him warmly.

Bill had been ill in Hawaii and was on his way home. He called the next morning from the L.A. airport. He was still running a fever, but the doctor had him on medication and he was eager to get home.

"Here's the new phone number," I told him, having just called the phone company to change the number so as to insure his rest.

"Just a minute," he replied. And I heard him say, "T, write this down."

And as I repeated it to Bill, he gave it to his companion, T. W. Wilson, who wrote it down.

I did not mention the visit from the F.B.I.

Late that night the silence was shattered by the phone ringing.

"Ruth," T. W.'s agitated voice came over the wire, "have you heard from Billy?"

"Not since this morning."

"No. I mean, do you know where he is?"

"With you, you nut," I replied, tired, and thinking he was trying to pull some sort of joke.

"No, before God, Ruth. He's not here."

Then I knew T. W. was dead serious.

"Not where?"

"With me. I'm here in Oteen. I had to stop for gas and I thought he might be thirsty and I asked him if he'd like me to get him something to drink. There was no answer so I opened the door to the back seat and the blanket and pillow were there, but no Billy!"

I felt myself go all numb and quiet inside.

"Back up, T," I said. "Tell me from the beginning."

Due to poor plane connections in Atlanta they had rented a car to drive home. Bill was made as comfortable as possible in the back seat with a pillow and blanket borrowed from a friendly Hilton Hotel manager. As T. W. drove, Bill soon fell asleep.

Later T. W. pulled into a truck stop at Jefferson, Georgia, to ask directions to the new freeway. It was pouring rain. Then, after getting the information, he opened the door quietly so as not to awaken Bill, eased himself behind the steering wheel, turned on the ignition, and started off—careful not to jerk the car. As they neared Greenville, South Carolina, T. W. asked in a low voice, just in case Bill should be waking up,

"Would you like to stop for something to drink?"

When there was no reply, he assumed Bill was still sleeping and drove through Greenville with care not to stop or start too suddenly at stoplights.

T. W. is an excellent driver under ordinary circumstances, and on the trip up the winding mountain road he must have set some sort of record for skillful maneuvering.

T. W. skirted Asheville, but at Oteen he realized they would not make the remaining ten miles without stopping for gas.

That's when he discovered the crumpled contents in the back seat contained no Bill.

"Come on up to the house," I suggested. "If for some reason he got out of the car, and you left, knowing Bill, he'll wait just a short while, then pay someone to drive him home."

As I waited for T. W. with Anne the silence in the house was deafening. Anne, wide awake and worried about her father, plied me with questions which I, too, was asking. I felt suspended in suspense. The silence throbbed.

I remembered the now ominous visit from the F.B.I. Had he

somehow been abducted? Anne knew nothing about that visit so at least did not have that possibility to worry about. I assured her that God was with her daddy.

I recalled Bill was on medication. What kind? Had he just sort of wandered off? Was he somewhere out in the night in the pouring rain, shivering with fever? The occasional flash of lightning followed by the growl and pounding of thunder did nothing to relieve the tension.

It was a relief to hear T. W.'s car coming up the drive. The rain had stopped.

We sat on the front steps talking, waiting, and not once, I am sure, had anyone for a moment stopped praying.

It was after one o'clock in the morning. In the distant darkness, we heard a car coming up the mountain. It seemed to take forever. And then he was there.

He parked. Got out of the car deliberately. Kissed me, then Anne, warmly. Nodded coolly at T. W. and walked past him into the house.

Undaunted, T followed us in, and his deep concern and overwhelming relief were so obvious, Bill thawed.

That first stop for gas in Georgia had awakened Bill, who thought it wise to take advantage of the rest room while there. As he emerged from the rest room he saw the taillights of the rented car disappearing up the road.

He paid a truck driver to catch up to him. T. W. is not only a superb driver—he's fast. The trucker returned, unsuccessful. So Bill walked into the small all-night cafe and ordered a cup of soup, thinking T. W. would realize his mistake and return any minute.

People eyed him suspiciously. These were farmers, truck drivers. Bill was dressed in traveling suit and tie, without a top coat, which was in the car. And the thunderstorm had not abated.

It was winter, and even the farmers were pale. Bill, fresh from Hawaii, was deeply tanned.

Finishing his cup of soup and T. W. not having returned, he went to the pay phone and placed a call to me. But the number

19

had been changed earlier, and the new one was in T. W.'s wallet.

"Is there a taxi around?" Bill asked.

"A taxi? Naw," the waiter scratched his jaw thoughtfully. "But there's a man down the road a piece with a car who drives folks sometimes."

Eventually the man appeared through the pouring rain and flashes of lightning and agreed to drive Bill to the Holiday Inn in Greenville for twenty dollars. Greenville was around one hundred miles further on, and looking at the cracked windshield and bent fenders, Bill hoped they would make it.

The driver eyed Bill suspiciously. In the rearview mirror he noticed the deeply tanned, well-dressed stranger without a top coat on a cold and rainy night, a man who kept watching the road for approaching lights, turning to look as each one passed (Bill was watching for T. W.).

They pulled up at Greenville's Holiday Inn around midnight. The night manager, recognizing Bill, warmly greeted him by name.

"You really are Billy Graham?" the driver asked. Bill acknowledged the fact.

"Law, I figured you were a hunted man with an eye out for the police! But you do resemble Billy Graham. Pleased to meet you," as he accepted his fare and shook Bill's hand warmly.

But the Holiday Inn was jammed. Not one room left. The manager was apologetic.

"Never mind," Bill said, "get me a rental car, and I'll drive home."

Which he did.

$\mathcal{3}$ ······ Journal

September 9, 1988

It is cool enough for a fire tonight, so I lit one in the bedroom fireplace. It both took the chill off the air and was company.

Bill left yesterday for Rochester, New York.

I had begun missing him the day before he left.

When he was walking to the plane, he was limping from that spider bite.

That should teach me not to laugh when he begins soaking what looked like a flea bite on his foot in hot Epsom salts. What I called hypochondria was more like intuition, for his foot began swelling by the hour. The doctor listened to Bill on the phone and agreed it wouldn't hurt to start taking antibiotics. So Bill found some in the medicine cabinet and began taking them.

When he got to Rochester, he was put in the hospital. No pain except when he walked. Only more swelling. They discovered staph and strep infections and prescribed intravenous doses of potent antibiotics every four hours, day and night.

Everyone is a bit in the dark—the general consensus was a brown recluse spider bite. Had he waited two or three days longer, he could have lost his foot, he was told reassuringly.

The fire is burning low now. It's nearly midnight and already the katydids have quit, except for an occasional chatter. This cold snap must have them confused. I love the all-engulfing antiphonal chattering of katydids from July till frost—each evening when darkness settles in, until sometime between midnight and dawn.

Anyway I am alone in this old house, with the dogs,

Pavarotti,* and the mate to that brown recluse spider. I have prayed and sprayed, and since I can keep in touch with Bill and the family by phone, and the Lord by prayer, I shall watch the firelight flickering on the old beamed ceiling and fall asleep, content.

*the canary

4 ······ Forgeries?

"I don't trust her," an older Christian observed of a newcomer to the household of God. "She's a phony." Strange, I thought to myself. Wouldn't the Father rather we welcomed a phony than put down a genuine new believer—however odd or difficult that new Christian might appear to be?

I thought of a man who was visiting Scotland Yard's counterfeit money department. "It must take years and years of studying counterfeits," he commented, "in order to know the real."

"Quite the contrary," came the reply. "It takes years and years of studying the real to make sure one can spot a counterfeit."

A former director of the Metropolitan Museum of Art in New York City is reputed to have said, *"Although it is a mistake to collect a fake, an error every adventurous connoisseur has made, it is an absolute sin to brand as a forgery an authentic work of art"* (THOMAS HOVING, *King of the Confessors*).

For us imperfect Christians, each at a different stage of our pilgrimage, it is even more difficult. Money, objects of art, books, paintings: all are completed, and static. But Christians, hopefully, are growing, even though in some that growth may be imperceptible. So the tests set forth by museum curators apply only in part.

Paul has given us the simplest common denominator, found in I Corinthians 12:3: *"No one can say 'Jesus is Lord' except by the Holy Spirit"* (RSV). Perhaps the Father watches how we welcome those who pass Paul's test—even though we might distrust them, might not like them because for some reason they fail to pass our own standards. But wouldn't we rather welcome a fake than brand as forgery an authentic work of grace?

5······Encouragement

Somewhere I came across the following:

"Let not this weak, unknowing hand
Presume Thy bolts to throw
And deal damnation round the land
On each I judge Thy foe."
—ALEXANDER POPE

God help us to be more welcoming, less judgmental; more encouraging, less critical.

The widow of George Dempster of London (*Finding Men for Christ, Touched By a Loving Hand, The Love That Will Not Let Me Go*) wrote me after his death that she was praying God would give her *"the ministry of encouragement."*

God has blessed certain of His servants with just such a ministry.

John Minder of Florida not only encouraged my husband when a student; he was an encourager to all young preachers who came across his path.

In England, Lindsey Glegg had such a ministry.

And Henrietta Mears of the First Presbyterian Church of Hollywood had such a ministry.

"More people fail through discouragement," someone has observed, *"than for any other reason."*

····· ⌘ ·····

Most families, it seems to me, have an encourager.

Not necessarily the oldest, youngest, or middle ones. They

seem to have an innate sense of balance, and a good sense of humor. These two qualities almost invariably go hand in hand.

They are the encouragers. They keep in touch by note or phone call. They smooth things over when the going gets a little rough. They aren't much on sharing their own problems or hurts because they are too busy shouldering those of others.

One family I know invariably turns to the youngest son—who is steady, unassuming, loyal, with remarkable wit and uncanny discernment. He is the family rallying point.

Andrew in the New Testament was a bit like this. He first brought his own brother, Peter, to Jesus (John 1:41). Then when there was no food for the five thousand, Andrew brought the lad with five loaves and two small fishes (John 6:8–9). When certain Greeks sought to see Jesus, it was Philip and Andrew who told Him. Andrew was the quiet disciple with the sensitive heart, quick to look for ways to help.

Our family has been blessed with five unique characters and each married to a unique character. Not a blob in the crowd. Plus nineteen grandchildren. No blobs there either.

But one in particular has been entrusted with this special gift of encouragement. That one will know of whom I am writing. *Thank you*, dear!

6······Falling Flat on One's Face

Who hasn't, at one time or another, fallen flat on one's face? Some people seem more prone to fall than others, more prone to failure.

I recall one baby Christian (a grown man, but a baby Christian) who, if I believed in reincarnation, I would have said was the apostle Peter back again—hot-tempered, big-hearted, impulsive.*

The older Christians were waiting for this man to fall. And it wasn't long before he obliged them.

He said later that the greatest stumbling block in the beginning of his Christian life was not his old drinking buddies, but skeptical Christians waiting for him to fall flat on his face so they could say, "I told you so!"

Many of us feel we have the gift of discernment when it comes to the faults and failures of other Christians—and on top of that, the gift of disapproval as well. But even our Lord came not to condemn (we were already condemned), *but that the world through him might be saved"* (JOHN 3:17).

"If a brother be overtaken in a fault [a different way of saying 'falling flat on one's face,' perhaps] *you who are spiritual restore such an one . . ."*

Who in your family or among your acquaintances do you most heartily disapprove of? Don't you think that one is already eaten up with guilt? How can you show kindness?

"The nicest thing we can do for our heavenly Father," wrote Saint Teresa of Avila, *"is to be kind to one of His children."*

---

*Stuart Hamblen died at 2:00 A.M. March 8, 1989.

7······The Art of Restoration

During World War II the city of Warsaw, Poland, was bombed for six years. The Nazis were determined to wipe it from the face of the earth. In a city of 3,500,000 only a handful crawled out of the rubble to greet the victorious German army when they arrived.

Later when the Nazis themselves had been defeated, the people who had fled to the countryside returned. Someone produced some old photographs. And with bare hands the Polish people began to rebuild the heart of their city stone by stone, lovingly, exactly. Where the former seven-hundred-year-old roof sagged, the reconstructed roof sagged. Today, standing in the center of this reconstructed area, one is easily transported back seven hundred years.

But here is the interesting thing: after the war when Germany had an old town or an old building which they wanted to restore, where did they look for help? To Polish artisans!

So your life has been devastated? God will give you the vision, strength, skill to rebuild. And with Him beside you the reconstruction can begin.

And who knows? Perhaps you will be permitted someday to use that art of restoration to help the very ones responsible for the devastation.

8······On Being "Chosen"

In college we had long, lively, and inconclusive debates on "free will" versus "predestination."

Then I read where John Newton told of an old woman who, on hearing a group of ministers discussing predestination, said, *"Ah! I have long settled that point; for if God had not chosen me before I was born, I am sure He would have seen nothing in me to have chosen me afterwards."*

9······Our Distance from God

"Our distance from God is that of inability to know and apprehend the near.

"It is the distance of the blind man from the glory of the picture in front of him;

"The distance of the deaf man from the beauty of the symphony sounding round about him.

"It is the distance of the insensate man from all the movements of life in the midst of which he lives."

—G. CAMPBELL MORGAN

10·····Is There Somewhere...?

Is there somewhere
—anywhere—
a little lonesome cabin
lost among the forests
on a wild, deserted shore;
an empty little cabin:
rough hewn, worn, and solid
with a dandy drawing chimney,
books, and windows—nothing more?
I'm tired of noise and traffic,
people pushing, phones and letters,
dates and deadlines, styles and headlines,
pride and pretense, nothing more;
and I'm needing such a cabin,
near God's masterpiece of mountains—
such a lost and lonesome cabin
where a tired soul can adore.

11 ······ "I Just Wanted to Hear Your Voice"

Once when out of the country, I called home to check on Mother and Daddy. After I talked with Daddy a few minutes, he said, "Here—your mother wants to say something." Since Mother's speech was affected by a stroke a number of years ago, I wondered how she would do. She came on the line, her voice weak, her spirit indomitable. "I just wanted to hear your voice," she managed to say.

Any wife with a husband on a trip, any mother with a child away from home, knows the longing for a letter (even a card), a call, . . . the sound of a loved voice. True, in prayer we are coming to Almighty God, the Creator of the universe, the King of kings and Lord of lords. He is also our Father. He longs to hear from us, not just when we are asking for things, but also to tell Him we love Him and to talk over the happenings of the day—just to hear a loved voice.

12·····God Rest You Merry...

"God rest you merry,
  gentlemen . . ."
and in these pressured days
I, too, would seek to be so blessed
by Him, who still conveys
His merriment, along with rest.
So I would beg, on tired knees,
"God rest me merry,
  please . . ."
              —R.B.G.
              One Christmas

13·····What a Year!

September 6, 1988

What a year!

Not from January 1, but from September 1987 to September 1988.

Bill and I have, aside from other appointments and things, traveled completely around the world twice in nine months.

We were in Tokyo on our way to China this time last year.

We had been in Helsinki where Bill had preached in the Olympic Stadium for six nights. Finland had had no summer. The weather was raw, cold, windy. Still the people came. Still they responded readily to the incredible message of redemption through Christ.

The last meeting Bill was suffering from vertigo as he preached—holding tightly to the pulpit as he felt the stadium circling about him. Those attending never knew.

After the closing night we flew to Copenhagen.

The next night we took the overnight over-the-North-Pole flight to Tokyo. Looking down at the North Pole from that height was awesome by moonlight. We glimpsed mountains and immense snow fields spread out endlessly—a lonely white vastness.

We landed in Anchorage, Alaska, for a brief refueling. The airport manager kindly greeted us and led us through the lovely big new airport to a quiet waiting room. Completely changed since I was there years ago.

When we arrived in Tokyo, Bill was suffering from jet lag, vertigo, an infection, and exhaustion.

I was having difficulty sleeping as concerned as I had been for years about the China trip, realizing Bill was unprepared— mentally, physically, or any way. It was only recently that he

33

realized Mr. Dung Hsiao Ping is Mr. Dung, not Mr. Ping. I wanted it to be a special trip. I was taking him to my birthplace, my old home, the land I loved in a unique way. And I could do nothing but pray.

Then one night he tripped over his briefcase and broke four ribs.

(For those traveling a great deal, it is wise to leave the bathroom light on at night and leave the door slightly ajar. Sleeping in a different room night after night makes it easy to get disoriented. And keep all briefcases out of the way!)

It was a painful experience for Bill. An enormous relief to me. Our Chinese hosts could not have been more gracious, understanding, or sympathetic. The trip was postponed till spring. (I did pray if it was not God's will then either, I sure hoped He would close the door a little more gently.)

We remained in Tokyo a few more days while Bill rested and healed a bit. That was exactly one year ago this time.

Each year, as I look back, has been jammed. Just one, noted in an old journal, listed:

Washington, D.C.
England
home
Mexico
Omaha, Nebraska
home
Omaha (surgery)
home
England
Switzerland
France
Germany
home
The Mayo Clinic
home
Omaha
The Mayo Clinic
Los Angeles

Omaha
Phoenix
Mesa
Florida
Saint Martin
Florida
home—with Christmas coming up, I hit the deck running.

And that was par for the course!

When I try to remember all that has happened before and since, I begin to feel like the "Packed Man."

14 ····· Packed Man

The man, asleep in the trash bin, was awakened with a jolt.

He had been scooped up along with the trash by a twenty-one-ton Indianapolis garbage truck.

Knocked unconscious, he came to upside-down and squeezed into an area where, as the driver later put it, "a human being shouldn't fit."

The truck started again and picked up two more loads of trash.

When the driver stopped for a third load, he heard some hollering.

Getting out, he looked around. The voice sounded far away, and he could see no one. So he started the compactor. That's when he heard a banging inside the truck. Thinking something mechanical was wrong, he stopped the cylinders.

Then, he later reported, he "heard a voice saying he sure would like to get out of wherever he was."

Fortunately, the driver saw to it that he did.

That was the way I have felt at times: too much to do, too far to go, and not enough time or strength to do it all, so that "you sure would like to get out of wherever you were."

"God does not promise strength for uncommanded work." Perhaps you're attempting things He hasn't commanded. When I began to feel compacted and cried for help, God showed me my priorities had gotten distorted. He was to come first. Then I realized I needed to be "liberated" from wherever I was: getting off boards and committees, writing no more books or articles for the time being, attending no unnecessary meetings, and accepting fewer outside responsibilities.

This was God's answer for me. He may have another solution for you.

I want to be liberated to be a wife, a homemaker, a mother, and a grandmother.

15·····One Step at a Time

Dodge Morgan started from Bermuda in *The Promise* sailing around the world alone.

"When I wasn't sure I could get through the day I knew I'd get through the next hour."

—DODGE MORGAN
Sunday, May 17, 1987

Listening to him, I realized for me, too, it was one hour at a time.
One event at a time.
One hour at a time.
One step at a time.

· · · · · ⌁ · · · · ·

As I was writing this, a church bulletin arrived in the morning mail from dearly loved Pastor Freyer in Mequon, Wisconsin, including the following which suited my situation exactly.

There was once a clock pendulum waiting to be fixed. It began to calculate how long it would be expected to tick day and night, so many times a minute, sixty times every hour, twenty-four hours every day, and three hundred and sixty-five times every year. It was awful! Enough to stagger the mind. Millions of ticks!

"I can never do it," said the poor pendulum. But the clockmaster encouraged it.

"Do just one tick at a time," he said. "That is all that will be required of you."

So the pendulum went to work, one tick at a time, and it is ticking yet.

16·····"Quite Magnificent!"

A friend was taking the children and me through the Bronx Zoo in New York. This friend being a V.I.P., the Zoo's Manager himself met and accompanied us.

Small Ned was pulling a tiny Matchbox car, tied to a long string. As we watched the monkeys, they were all watching Ned and his tiny car with great curiosity.

Then we came to the cage with the baboons.

As could be expected, even little Ned's interest and curiosity were aroused. The children were fascinated, amused, and vocal about the fact that that particular portion of the anatomy upon which the baboons sat (which we usually referred to as the "back porch") was a brilliant red. Our hostess and I were looking elsewhere and commenting on other things.

Not the children.

And I heard the Zoo's Manager say to them, kindly and with dignity,

"For a baboon, that is considered quite magnificent!"

I never forgot it.

17·····"Glory Coming Up"

On our daily trips to check on the progress of our new house up the mountain, the children and I noticed a bulge in the pavement. The road was new, and the pavement fresh and unbroken.

What, we wondered, had the nerve and strength to push its way up and through six inches of road binding and four inches of asphalt? Each day the little mound rose noticeably, and the children were full of ideas.

"It's an oak tree."

"No. It's a locust."

"No, dummy, it's a walnut."

"I know," I heard little Bunny exclaim, "it's a morning glory—and that's the glory coming up!"

You see that in people, especially baby believers in Christ. Or perhaps it is just more noticeable in them. Anyway, Christ's life comes through. And we, too, can say, "It's the glory coming up!"

P.S. It turned out to be a mushroom.

18·····Big Man

"It takes a big man to be willing to do a little job, where there is a need."

In the winter of 1971, we were spending a few weeks in Florida. Bill joined us when he could.

Our oldest daughter, Gigi, and her husband, Stephan, were flying down to weekend with us.

The nearest airport was Melbourne, Florida.

The plane was due after dark, and Bill, busy with another appointment, asked Lee Fisher, a longtime friend, to drive me.

We carried T. W.'s suitcase and golf clubs which he had left in Florida, and which he wanted us to air freight to him in North Carolina.

"Drop me with the suitcase and clubs at the entrance," I said to Lee, as the only parking allowed was in the lot just across the street. "I'll get a porter to carry them to air freight for me."

As Lee drove off, I spotted two young men sitting on a bench near the door.

"Would one of you mind taking these to the air freight counter for me?" I asked.

"Sure," one replied and, securing a cart, lifted the bags aboard.

At the counter I learned air freight was closed for the weekend.

Just then, Lee walked in. Explaining the situation to him, I suggested he have the porter put the bags back in the car, adding,

"I tipped him on the way in. You tip him on the way out."

Then I went into the little coffee shop to get a cup of coffee while waiting for the plane to arrive.

Lee joined me shortly, chuckling.

"You sure know how to pick them!"

"Pick what?"

"Pick porters." And he started laughing.

"What do you mean?"

"When we got to the car, I tried to tip him and he refused, saying you had already given him too much. I said, 'You don't look like a porter to me,' and he said, 'I'm not.'

"'What do you do for a living?' I asked.

"'I pitch for the Minnesota Twins.'"

Still laughing, Lee got up and left the coffee shop.

In a few minutes he was back with "The Porter."

"Ruth," Lee said, "I'd like to you meet Al Metz, pitcher for the Minnesota Twins."

19 ····· The Executioner

In 1900 in China the Boxer Rebellion erupted with the blessing of the Dowager Empress, Tz'u-hsi.

Orders went out from the Foreign Legations that all westerners were to proceed quickly to places of safety. As many as possible were to go to Shanghai or Peking. The rest were to go to their Provincial Capitals and seek political asylum from the Governor of the Province until the storm had blown over.

The Rev. James R. Graham hurried his wife, Sophie, and their three children down to Shanghai.

There, daily reports arrived of a missionary killed here, a family there, some faithful Chinese Christians brutally murdered by the Boxers in another town. The missionaries, gathered in safety, lived from report to report with heavy hearts.

Graham wondered about his friend of the Bible Society, Mr. Whitehouse, and his young bride of two weeks. They had been in Shansi Province. Were they safe?

Then came the blackest day of all. Between forty-six and a hundred missionaries from the Northern Provinces had sought refuge in the Governor's courtyard at the Provincial Capital, Taiyuanfu in Shansi, not knowing the Governor was a leader of the Boxer uprising. They had all been executed.

The question "why?" trembled on the lips of more than one brave missionary. The need had been so great, and now this waste. Numb with grief they awaited details. But the only news filtered through by word of mouth from someone, who had been told by someone, who had been told . . .

Weeks dragged past. Gradually the fury of the storm spent itself, and in the grim stillness that followed, Graham returned alone to Tsingkiang, nearly three hundred miles north on the Grand Canal, to see if it was safe enough for the others to return.

．．．．． ◈ ．．．．．

Shortly after his arrival in Tsingkiang, Uncle Jimmy had a visitor.

The story this visitor told Uncle Jimmy (as he was known to us all) is perhaps the first eyewitness account of the Shansi massacre. He, in turn, told it to me in 1942, while visiting in Montreat. I wrote it down that night. Uncle Jimmy was to have married Bill and me the next year, but he died three months before the wedding.

．．．．． ◈ ．．．．．

Few stopped to notice the stranger as he made his way down the narrow streets carefully avoiding the puddles. It was night, and the lamps had been lit in the little shops. Rickshaws and wheelbarrows, dogs and people everywhere. At the little tea shop overlooking the canal, he stopped to inquire his way. Was there a foreigner in the town? No. He with his family had moved to Shanghai when the trouble broke out. Someone spoke up. The foreigner had returned a few days ago, alone. Where did he live? Up the street a little way—turn here, turn there. At the end of the little alley is a gate. Bang loudly. The gateman is deaf. The stranger thanked them briefly. And those in the tea shop speculated after he had gone. From the north, by his speech, Shansi most likely. And they went back to sucking in their boiling tea.

．．．．． ◈ ．．．．．

"Coming," mumbled the gateman, pulling on his jacket and shuffling out of his room. Then louder, as the knocking continued insistently, "Coming! Coming! Who is it?" Receiving no reply but an imperious "Open the gate!" he slid back the heavy wooden bolt and peered through the crack. "Who is it?"

45

"Is the foreigner at home?"

"Wait a minute . . ."

And bolting the door in the stranger's face, he hurried within.

"I do not like his looks. He has an evil face," he informed the missionary. "I do not like his way. He is from the north. And if you tell me, I will say it is late and you do not wish to be disturbed."

"No," the missionary said. "Let him in and pour some tea."

Grumbling, the gateman obeyed. Shortly, he ushered the stranger into the simple living quarters. He was an ordinary looking man with an extraordinarily hard face. In spite of his authoritative bearing, he appeared nervous. The preliminary greetings over, he inquired what lay behind the door to the right. "The bedroom," replied the missionary.

"What lies in there?" pointing his chin to the adjoining door.

"The kitchen."

"What is in there?" his chin jerked toward the next door.

"Just a minute," replied the missionary (his "dander up" as he described it later). "This is my home and you are my guest. It is none of your affair what lies beyond these doors."

Hastily the stranger apologized for his rudeness, adding that he was only wanting to make sure they were alone as he had some business of a very private nature to discuss.

Assured they were absolutely alone, he proceeded.

"Do you remember the foreigners who sought protection at Taiyuanfu with Yu Hsien, Governor of Shansi Province?"

"I have heard."

"You have heard." The stranger sat silent a few minutes. "I was there," he added.

"You saw them die?"

"I am captain of Yu Hsien's bodyguard. I was in charge."

"You were responsible?" But something in the man's face—so hard, so hopeless—stopped him. He could have told him what he thought. He could have lashed out at him with all the grief and indignation in him. But something sealed his lips and kept him waiting silently for the captain to proceed.

46

"I was following instructions," he continued. "To me, at the time, it was nothing. I am a man accustomed to killing. Another life—ten, twenty, one hundred. It was nothing . . . .

"Yu Hsien, the Governor of Shansi Province, he does not like foreigners. He does not like them, nor their ways, nor their doctrine. When they began to gather at his door asking for protection in the name of their government, his soul rankled within him. 'Protection? I can only protect you by putting you in the prison,' he replied, harshly.

"So he put them in prison. For several days he kept them there while his hatred grew. Then he called me in and gave me my orders. I am a man trained to obey, and I am a man accustomed to killing. These foreigners—I cared not one way or the other.

"We led them out into the prison courtyard and lined them up. Yu Hsien was there and berated them loudly and angrily. 'I do not like you foreigners,' he shouted. 'I do not like you, or your ways or your foreign teaching.' Then he told them they were all to be killed."

He paused again—struggling for words. The missionary was sitting forward, scarcely breathing. "Go on. Go on," he urged. "What happened next?"

"Then happened the strangest sight I have ever witnessed. There was no fear. Husbands and wives turned and kissed one another. When the little children, sensing something terrible about to happen, began to cry, their parents put their arms about them and spoke to them of 'Yesu,' pointing up toward the heavens and smiling.

"Then they turned to face their executioners, calmly as though this thing did not concern them. They began singing. And singing they died.

"When I saw how they faced death," he hurried on, "I knew this 'Yesu' of whom they spoke was truly God.

"But tell me. Can God forgive my so-great sin?"

The missionary thought of his close friend, Whitehouse, and his bride of a few weeks, who had been among those killed. He thought of others.

The captain was speaking again. "I am at present on my way

escorting Yu Hsien's wife to the northeast. Tonight we rest in this city. Tomorrow we continue our journey. I sought you out, foreigner, to ask you—is there nothing, nothing I might do to atone for my wrong? Is there nothing?"

A Hand was on the missionary's heart as he thought to himself, Can God forgive? What of Christ on the cross praying, "Father, forgive"? What of Saul of Tarsus who kept the clothes of those who stoned young Stephen and persecuted those of the way "beyond measure"? What of him?

The officer sat silent, waiting. The missionary reached for his worn Chinese Bible. "Listen," he found himself saying. "Our God, whom we serve, is a merciful God. True, your sin was great. Very great. But His mercy is even greater. This Jesus is His Son who came to earth to die for sinners like you. I, too, am a sinner. All men are sinners. And because He died for you, for Jesus, His Son's sake, God can forgive you."

The captain listened closely. Foreign words these, to a mind schooled to hate, to kill—but not to forgive. He drank in every strange word. "Love . . . Forgive . . . Life." He listened. The little he could understand, he accepted, simply, asking an occasional question and again listening closely.

It was late when the missionary escorted the captain to the gate and bowed farewell. It was the last he saw or heard of him.

• • • • • ⌬ • • • • •

The missionary sat a long while thinking. Fresh in his mind were hundreds of new graves strewn across China like wheat sown at random.

No more the anguished, "Lord, why this great waste?"

The harvest had begun.

• • • • • ⌬ • • • • •

$\mathcal{20}\cdots$ Remember Your Position

The local sheriff had decided to tighten the requirements for his deputies. Each man had to qualify on the firing range, and the distance had been extended from fifteen yards to twenty-five yards. So the deputies gathered to try their hand at hitting the target at the increased distance. Each man had eighteen seconds to get off twelve shots.

The best shot in the area is also a personal friend, George Burgin, who, together with his wife, Corenne, keeps an eye on Bill and me. The day before the trials he had been fitted with his first pair of trifocals. When his time came to shoot, he drew a bead on the target.

"Suddenly," as he told me later, "I began to perspire. And when I perspire, my glasses fog up. There I was with a bead drawn on the target, and all I could see was fog.

"Then I remembered what our old Navy instructor had taught us: 'If (for some reason) you ever lose sight of the target,' he said, 'just remember your position.'

"So," our friend said, "I just held my position and pulled the trigger as fast as I could. By then I had less than eighteen seconds, but I got off all twelve shots. When I took off my glasses and wiped them, I had hit the bull's-eye every time."

There are times when we, for some reason, lose sight of our target—which is to glorify our Lord. The world is too much with us. Tears blur our vision. Unexplained tragedy raises questions that cannot be answered and shakes our faith to its foundations.

Then we must remember our position, for the Christian's position is "in Christ." As if we were tired or hurt children, He will gather both us and our loads.

Though we may not, for some reason, see the target, if we just "remember our position," we won't miss.

21 ····· Tadpole Soup

A few friends joined us for supper that spring. Lee Fisher was among them.

We started with clear consommé containing tiny meatballs.

Now, it was tadpole season, and the temptation was irresistible.

In Lee's soup bowl we put water, colored to match the consommé, and tadpoles to match the meatballs.

Everyone was seated, the blessing had been asked, and we started on the first course. Only when Lee tried to spoon up a meatball, it swam away from him.

22 ···· The Awful Patient Ways of God

Genesis 12:2, 4—Isaac is promised to the childless couple, Abraham and Sarah (Abraham is then seventy-five years old). After ten years Abraham grows impatient and takes Hagar, Sarah's maid (a custom permitted in those days), and has a son, Ishmael (Genesis 16). Abraham was one hundred when God's promise was finally fulfilled (Genesis 21:3, 5), and Isaac was born.

· · · · · ❦ · · · · ·

Joseph, falsely accused by Potiphar's wife, had been imprisoned. After Joseph correctly interpreted the dreams of the butler and the baker, the butler promised to remember Joseph when he was restored. But he forgot.

Many never live to see their prayers answered.

"And it came to pass at the end of two full years . . . ," he remembered and Joseph was freed.

· · · · · ❦ · · · · ·

"And it came to pass in process of time" (Exodus 2:23) that Pharaoh died and the children of Israel sighed, cried, and groaned *"by reason of the bondage* . . . And God heard . . . [and] remembered . . . [and] had respect unto them."

Yet it was forty years before He sent Moses back to lead them out. (Compare Acts 7:23 with Exodus 7:7.)

· · · · · ❦ · · · · ·

Samuel anointed David king when David was but a boy (I Samuel 16:13). But it was not for ten or fifteen years that he was finally crowned (II Samuel 2). Note David's behavior during those years.

God drafted Jeremiah to prophesy judgment and the destruction of Jerusalem in the thirteenth year of Josiah's reign. But it was forty years and three months before Jerusalem was finally destroyed.

Jesus, at twelve years of age, stayed behind in the Temple, both asking and answering questions. When found by His parents and reproached, He replied, *"Wist ye not that I must be about my Father's business?"* But He returned with them to Nazareth *"and was subject unto them."* It was eighteen years before He began His public ministry.

"And therefore will the Lord wait, that he may be gracious unto you . . . He will be very gracious."
—ISAIAH 30:18–19

"Are we prepared to take the awful patient ways of God, we must not be infected by the world's valuation of either speed or success."
—JOHN B. PHILLIPS

"Wait on the Lord . . ." Or as the Prayer Book version translates it, *"O, tarry thou the Lord's leisure"* —PSALM 27:14. And He is so leisurely sometimes!
"I waited patiently for the Lord . . ."
—PSALM 40:1

And, comments George Mathison, *"that is the grandest patience in the universe."*

23 · · · · Morning Song

I had been getting up early, fixing myself a cup of coffee, and then sitting in the rocker on the front porch while I prayed for each of our children, and for each of theirs.

One morning I awoke earlier than usual. It was five o'clock, with dawn just breaking over the mountains. I collected my cup of coffee and settled into the old rocker. Suddenly, I realized a symphony of bird song was literally surrounding me. The air was liquid with music, as if the whole creation were praising God at the beginning of a new day. I chuckled to hear the old turkey gobbler, that had recently joined our family, gobbling away down in the woods at the top of his voice as if he were a song sparrow!

And I learned a lesson. I had been beginning my days with petitions, and I should have been beginning them with praise.

When the disciples asked our Lord to teach them how to pray, He gave them what we commonly know as the Lord's Prayer. The very first line is one of praise: *"Hallowed be thy name."*

In the seventeenth century, John Trapp wrote: *"He lets out His mercies to us for the rent of our praise, and is content that we may have the benefit of them so He may have the glory."*

24 · · · · Such Unorchestrated Music

Such
unorchestrated music
one has seldom heard:
dawn breeze
in the tops of trees,
much
liquid song of bird:
sparrow,
robin,
towhee,
indigo bunting—
wren,
meadow lark
and cardinal,
mockingbird,
finch
and when
my soul is on its tiptoes,
filled with ecstasy,
the turkey gobbles loudly
down by the locust tree.

25 · · · · Enjoy Your Work?

The weather has been a record heat breaker.

The local evening news showed a couple of house painters patiently, perspiringly applying paint to a frame house. The commentator warned of the danger of heat stroke working in the hot sun.

Later on the same program they showed the tennis tournament at a local country club. But no word of warning here.

Playing hard on a hot day is fine—but be careful how you work!

· · · · · ∽⧉∼ · · · · ·

U.S. Championship, New York, 1988

Just now I am watching the Lendl-Wilander tennis match— When they started, they were clean shaven. Now, four hours later, Wilander is growing a beard.

It is now after 9:00 P.M.—brilliant, brutal, incredibly skillful playing. Wilander won after four hours and fifty-nine minutes. A U.S. record.

If they had been forced to do it, the world would call it torture.

I think it's the way one looks at things. It's enjoying what you're doing that makes the difference.

Not that all of life is to be fun.

Mr. Sam Means had a large ranch in Texas.

He had ridden horses all his life. His legs were literally bowed to the shape of a horse. He was a special friend of Grady Wilson and came with him to one of the crusades.

Just to make conversation at lunch one day, I asked,

"Do you enjoy horseback riding?"

He looked at me in amusement.

"Law!" he exclaimed. "I never rode a horse for pleasure in my life!"

26 ···· Tennis Is Work?

Several years ago I was watching on French TV the men's tennis championship final at Wimbledon, England: it was Borg versus McEnroe.

In the background, behind the almost constant chatter of French commentators, one could hear the calm and incisive, yet brief remarks of the British announcer stating the score from time to time, and with equally detached coolness saying occasionally, "Quiet, please, so the players can concentrate."

I think of the hours of training, the worldwide attention, the lifetime dedication to the sport: this is not a game of relaxation.

Then I recalled the early days of missionary work in China. The missionaries, among whom I was brought up, were deeply committed, highly qualified, and well trained, and they believed that relaxation was an essential part of hard work. So they built a tennis court—dirt, of course, not grass as at Wimbledon. And they played for fun.

Occasionally they even had an audience. One afternoon, two Chinese gentlemen stopped by in the middle of a game. With hands tucked up their sleeves, Oriental fashion, they watched first with interest, then with growing concern. As the game drew to a conclusion and the overheated players, mopping their foreheads, joined their Chinese friends, they were greeted with genuine sympathy.

"We were talking together," they said, feeling their way so as not to offend. "Wondering, can you Americans not afford to hire people to bat that ball back and forth for you?"

27····Depth Fish

A mutilated blob floated on the surface of the ocean. "A depth fish," explained the captain of the small fishing boat.

There are fish living so far beneath the ocean surface that when one happens to be caught and hauled to the surface along with the rest of the fisherman's catch, it is unable to exist without the pressure that holds it together: it simply explodes.

There are people like this. They live continually under incredible pressure. But when, for some reason, that pressure is removed, they fall apart.

Newspapers have told us of musicians, artists, and writers, dissidents expelled from their homeland now living in some neutral country. And some have become unproductive.

Much has been written about tension, pressure, and friction—mostly on ways to escape them. We have become a generation of escape artists.

J. N. Darby translates Psalm 4:1 thus: *"In pressure Thou has enlarged me."* William Barclay tells us the Greek word for *affliction* (as in II Corinthians 6:4) means *"pressures."* They are, he says, *"the things which press sore upon us. Originally it expressed sheer physical pressure on a man . . . The sheer pressure of the demands of life upon one."*

28···· *Pressures*

There are **pressures** and PRESSURES. *This* is about necessary, even creative pressure: not pressure that destroys and debilitates. Capstones, not compactors.

Have you ever studied an old stone arch? The capstone supports the weight of the whole: it bears the pressure.

We appreciate the value of pressure when we see a tourniquet applied stopping the flow of blood and thus saving a life.

J. Hudson Taylor, that great pioneer missionary to China, used to say we should not mind how great the pressure is—only where the pressure lies. If we make sure it never comes between us and our Lord, then the greater the pressure, the more it presses us to Him.

Actor Dustin Hoffman says of director Mike Nichols, "*Mike has grace under pressure*" (*Look* MAGAZINE, APRIL 2, 1968). What a lovely thing to have said of one!

Perhaps our secret of "*grace under pressure*" lies in accepting that pressure as from the Lord. At least permitted by Him.

It may be one more request than we think we can fulfill, one more responsibility than we think we can manage, one more phone call, one more pile of dishes to wash, one more bed to make, one more room to clean, one more complaint to listen to, one more interruption . . .

"*Interruptions never distracted Jesus. He accepted them as opportunities of a richer service.*

"*Interruptions were the occasion of some of His most gracious deeds and revealing words.*"

—G. H. MORLING
Quest For Serenity

Yet, as we accept it as from Him, asking Him to teach us what He would have us learn through the experience and to use it for the good of others and for His glory, pressure will have fulfilled its purpose.

An old copy of the *London Times* has this thought-provoking statement: *"The grace of final perseverance is that quality of patience which is always equal to the pressure of the passing moment, because it is rooted in that eternal order over which the passing moment has no power."*

29 · · · · He Went into the Temple

He went into the Temple
then,
casting out all who bought
and sold,
upsetting seats of the money men
trading the gifts of God
for gold.
And when
the outraged cries
had died,
and He stood alone
on that battle-field,
the blind and lame,
who came to Him there,
were healed.

· · · · · ～〇～ · · · · ·

Lord of this temple,
commandeered
by alien interests,
let Your voice,
feared,
thunder with fury
throughout the whole;
Your whip be felt
on alien backs
till all have crept

into the night;
my shambled soul,
cleansed and still,
once more put right,
shall wait for You alone
to fill
it with Your love,
Your light.
And those in need
may come to find
help for the crippled,
sight for the blind.

30 ···· They Say You've Gone to Heaven

They say You've gone to heaven, but I have heard them tell
that before You went to heaven, Lord, You also went to hell.
So come down Lord from Your heaven, for if You went to hell
come down into the clip joint, Lord, come down to us as well.

Smoke rises in Your churches to praise Your holiness
smoke rises from our reefers to cloud our loneliness,
so come down from Your heaven, to call, to heal, to bless,
You know that our smoke rings are signals of distress.

With publicans and sinners they say You often dined,
they say a girl who was a tart with You found peace of mind.
So come down Lord from Your heaven, for if You love our kind
come down into the strip club, Lord, where only love is blind.

The sick—they need a doctor more than the healthy do
they say You took a dying thief to paradise with You
so come down from Your heaven if what they say is true
come down to the den of thieves where thieves have need of You.

They say You were victorious over hell and over death,
we know the hell of heroin, the dying that is meth,
so come down from Your heaven, You whom we can't confess
and be the resurrection of this our living death.

P.S. Written by a girl in Soho, London, a heroin addict
who died.

Had any ideas lately?

31·····TM

A lot has been said and written lately about Transcendental Meditation.

According to the dictionary, *transcendental* is an adjective describing a very high and remarkable degree; surpassing, excelling. The philosopher would say it is something that lies beyond the bounds of all personal experience and knowledge. The theologian would define it as lying above and beyond the universe. It is used of God Himself.

So I went to my Reference Point, the Bible, and, with the aid of a concordance, looked up every reference for *meditate*. I discovered they fall into four categories.

We are to meditate on:

God Himself—all that He is.

All that God has done.

All that God has said.

All that God has commanded.

What could be more strengthening, more reassuring, than this kind of Transcendental Meditation?

32 · · · · Someone in the Gutter

"When we see someone in the gutter with the footprints of the devil all over him, you may just stop and think 'How much God must love him!' Because, you see, the devil doesn't bother with those who aren't particularly dear to God. Satan hates God, and the only way he can attack God is by attacking the objects of His love."

—SOPHIE GRAHAM
Daughter of the missionary
James R. Graham

33 · · · · Media Manipulation

"A beast does not know that he is a beast, and the nearer a man gets to being a beast the less he knows it."

—GEORGE MACDONALD

· · · · · ∽➢◡ · · · · ·

"Vice is a monster of so frightful mien,
As to be hated needs but to be seen;
Yet seen too oft, familiar with her face,
We first endure, then pity, then embrace."
—ALEXANDER POPE

· · · · · ∽➢◡ · · · · ·

Do I embrace today what shocked me yesterday?

34 · · · · Hearing the Cheers

I have often wondered why basketball has not made a tremendous hit in England. Due to the weather, one would think it would be an ideal sport. But from what we have heard, there is little or no place for an audience to sit, and no enthusiasm has ever been engendered for this particular sport. It makes one wonder how important it is for players to hear the reaction of the crowd.

"Wherefore seeing we also are compassed about with so great a cloud of witnesses, let us lay aside every weight, and the sin which doth so easily beset us, and let us run with patience the race that is set before us, looking unto Jesus the author and finisher of our faith."
—HEBREWS 12:1–2

These verses have just been preceded by the great roll call of faith in Hebrews 11. And the picture I get is of a great stadium in which are seated all the saints who have preceded us, watching our progress as well as those listed in chapter 11. And I know that there are times in my own life when I have thought, If only I could hear one cheer!

35····Compassed About

"Compassed about
with a great cloud—"
the Scriptures say;
—if only I could hear
one shout—
the distant roar
of that great crowd—
just some small word—
aloud—
      aloud—
to cheer my way.

36···· Running

Sixteen thousand!

Beneath our hotel window, across the street, the cheering and shouts of encouragement reverberated throughout New York City.

It was the annual Marathon, and sixteen thousand contestants were gamely galloping through Central Park that year.

All day from mid-morning on. And still they came. And the cheering was without letup.

That verse quoted in a previous chapter, *"Let us run with patience the race that is set before us,"* describes it.

That's it. It's running with patience. Sometimes painful, dogged determination rather than speed seems the essence of these popular marathons.

These people run for the joy of running. Dr. Richard Gieser of Wheaton, Illinois (whose father and mother served with us in China, where his father interned in the hospital), runs in these marathons for the fun of it.

Others run for the joy of it, too. Like Eric Liddel of *Chariots of Fire.*

And Stan Cottrell. He has run across America. He ran across Scotland (where we had put him in touch with Eric Liddel's sister) to Gibraltar (I would love to have been a sea gull to watch him run across The Channel!). He ran across the Dominican Republic. He ran across China (Beijing to Guangzhou). To name a few runs.

"Where have you been recently?" I asked over the phone.

"I ran across Vietnam."

"What was it like?"

"Poor," he said. "You've never seen such poverty. But friendly. I never saw an unfriendly face."

"And where next?" I asked.

"North Korea," came the reply. "Only they won't let me run to the D.M.Z. Just around Pyong Yang."

Pyong Yang, I thought to myself, was where I had gone to high school. The world is growing smaller.

Some days I can't run. I do well to get out of bed.

37 ···*Against All Odds*

Vero Beach
Spring 1971
The little plane lifted off the runway, disappearing into the light cloud cover.

The next day Franklin called from school to say they had arrived safely, adding matter-of-factly that they had had some trouble on the way and had to make a forced landing in Jackson. Nothing more.

So when Calvin Booth, his flight instructor, wrote, we opened his letter eagerly. Racing through his opening remarks, we came to . . .

"You are probably still a bit hazy as to the details surrounding our return trip, so I will seek to briefly cover the events.

"The odds are probably at least one in ten thousand against this particular failure, but I feel that the Lord placed us in this position to prove His goodness and constant care in a very dynamic way.

"A check of enroute weather at Mobile revealed an area of thunderstorm activity across southern Mississippi and Louisiana so we decided to go north to Jackson and west to Longview. This course took us over a number of larger cities with lighted airports, whereas a direct flight would have taken us over a sparsely settled area in Mississippi and Louisiana. In the area of Jackson, while flying in the overcast, the generator failed and the battery ran down, leaving us without lights, navigation, or communication capability. A quick prayer provided the necessary calmness and we decided to descend out of the cloud and look for Jackson, as we were only thirty or forty miles west of there. Frank and I were mutually thankful for each other and I have only praise for his help and performance during that seemingly endless fifteen or twenty minutes.

"When safely settled on the ground, we went up to the tower to express our appreciation for what we thought was a great deal of help on their part, only to find that they didn't even know we were around until they saw us on the runway. We were thrilled to see the miracles unfold as the controllers told us that they were demonstrating the airport lighting system to a couple of visitors at the time. They had turned the lights up to full brilliance just as we approached the field and also turned on the flashing strobes which we thought to mean indication of their assistance. We were happy to see the lights and were even happier to be on the ground.

"It seems that Franklin is getting more than his fair share of learning experiences lately, but I can assure you that this was a very worthwhile experience for him as well as for his instructor. A lesson learned under this type of circumstance is not soon forgotten. I think that something like this is good from time to time as it renews our awareness of God's role as guardian of our lives."

To what extent God had guarded them that night, we did not learn until four years later.

During the Jackson crusade, someone sent my husband a newspaper article from Jackson dated April 15, 1971, by Wilbur M. Irwin, Pastor, Forest Hill, Jackson.

". . . Gary Cornett, minister of music at Forest Hill Baptist Church, and his wife, Pat, had arrived at the airport at Sydney's invitation to see the various operations. They were allowed to go up into the tower, and Sydney began demonstrating the various equipment. He had received a call from Memphis concerning the small plane but assumed that they had made contact with each other and passed on to other matters. Sydney demonstrated a light-gun which has tri-colored lights. He turned on the red light and a white light while the gun remained inside the tower, but for an unexplained reason he held the gun out the window when he demonstrated the green light and said, 'If I were going to give a pilot clearance to land I would point this light directly at him and turn the green light on.' A fellow worker asked Sydney if he would demonstrate the run-way lights. Sydney started to turn them on, and gradually they got brighter and brighter until they reached the state of high-intensity. The latter degree of lighting is for

*emergency, and the lights are designed to pierce fog and clouds to give
pilots in emergency situations a view of the run-ways.*

"Sydney had scarcely completed these demonstrations when his
co-worker said in excitement, 'There is an unlighted plane coming in.'
Sydney responded, 'There isn't a plane within 50 miles of us in the air.'
Upon closer examination with the aid of binoculars it was quickly
learned that an unlighted single-engine plane was coming in for a
landing.

". . . In one sense Sydney McCall was demonstrating the lighting
and signal system to Gary Cornett, but the pilot of that plane is
positive that God's providential Hand was in it all. He commented,
'God's hand was in it. You see, we just left Billy Graham there in
Florida and he prayed for our safety before we departed.'"

The writer of that article did not know who the copilot of
that little plane was.

• • • • • ∽⌒⌒⌒∾ • • • • •

"I think that something like this is good from time to time."
Calvin Booth, Franklin's flight instructor, had written us after
that flight,

". . . it renews our awareness of God's role as guardian of our
lives."

• • • • • ∽⌒⌒⌒∾ • • • • •

The following year Calvin Booth was killed in a plane crash.

38 · · · · Unexplained Tragedy

"I have been thinking of how many unexplained things there are in life. Our Lord Jesus who could have explained everything, explained nothing. He said there would be tribulation, but He never said why. Sometimes He spoke of suffering being to the glory of God, but He never said how. All through the scriptures it is the same. I cannot recall a single explanation of trial. Can you? We are trusted with the unexplained."

A. W. CARMICHAEL
Edges of His Ways

· · · · · ∽∾ · · · · ·

I lay my "whys"
before Your Cross
in worship kneeling,
my mind too numb
for thought,
my heart beyond
all feeling.

And worshipping,
realize that I
in knowing You
don't need a "why."

I was tucking a small Ned in bed one night long ago. Something he had seen on television or had heard being discussed was bothering him.

"What if something bad happens to us?" he asked. I reminded him that God is all-powerful and that nothing can touch a child of God without God's permission.

"Yes," he countered, "but what if God gives His permission?"

"In that case," I said, "it is His will which is 'good, and acceptable, and perfect.'"

Satisfied, he went to sleep.

39 · · · · *Away—Or Up?*

I remember once when troubles descended like a sudden storm that dumps ten inches of rain in twenty-four hours. But why is it that way? Why do troubles so often come in bunches or in such rapid succession that we barely have time to catch our breath before another downpour?

I'm glad the psalmist did not live on a perpetual high. David once longed for wings of a dove so that he might fly away and be at rest. We would settle for the wings of a Concorde or a 747—even a Piper Cub!

Then I discovered God's promise in Isaiah 40:31. There, those who *"wait upon the Lord shall renew their strength; they shall mount up with wings as eagles; they shall run, and not be weary; and they shall walk, and not faint."*

So it boils down to: "Away"—or "up"? The key seems to be "waiting on the Lord."

In this "instant" generation most of us don't wait easily. But we can learn. F. B. Meyer once wrote: *"Not always talking to Him or about Him but waiting before Him till the stream runs clear, till the cream rises to the top; till the mists part and the soul regains its equilibrium."*

Jeremiah, in the most dismal of circumstances, wrote: *"The Lord is good unto them that wait for Him"* (LAMENTATIONS 3:25).

· · · · · ~⌒~ · · · · ·

"Sunshine is a matter of altitude."

—F. W. BOREHAM

40 ···· Exchange of Love

"Am I not enough, Mine own? Enough
Mine own, for Thee?
All Thou shalt find at last
Only in Me.
Am I not enough, Mine own?
I, forever and alone,
I needing Thee?"
　　　　—TER STEEGAN
　　　　Translated from
　　　　the Old German

· · · · · ∽⟨⟩∾ · · · · ·

"Lord, Thou art life, tho' I be dead;
Love's fire Thou art, however cold I be.
Nor heaven have I, nor place to lay my head,
Nor home but Thee."
　　　　　　—CHRISTINA ROSSETTI

#1 ····· Salty Christians

It happened in one of those countries whose leaders deny the existence of God but allow the church to exist under a secretary for church affairs. In this case, the secretary was not only a brilliant pastor, he was a medical doctor as well.

One day he was called on the carpet by the authorities. Knowing there would be a new crackdown on the Christians, he started right in: "I know you gentlemen wish to interrogate me," he began. "But first, may I say something?"

Permission granted, he continued. "You know I am a medical doctor. I know the importance of salt in the human body: it should be maintained at about 2 percent. If it is less, a person gets sick. If it is eliminated altogether, he will die.

"Now, Jesus Christ has said Christians are the salt of the earth." Then he paused. "That is all. And now, gentlemen, what is it that you wish to say to me?"

"Oh, nothing, nothing . . . ," they agreed. And he was dismissed.

We do not know when salt was first discovered, but Numbers 18:19 refers to the *"covenant of salt."* The Greeks had a saying, *"Trespass not against the salt and the board."* An Arab saying went, *"There is salt between us."* In Ezra 4:14, the expression *"to eat the salt of the palace"* is used. The modern Persian phrase *namak haram,* "untrue to salt," means to be disloyal or ungrateful. In English, *the salt of the earth* commonly describes someone who is both loved and trusted.

Salt is indispensable to man's health and is fed to livestock for the same reason (see the *Encyclopaedia Britannica*). It is also used as a preservative and for seasoning, as well as in curing hides and as brine for refrigeration. But there is another fact about salt that is worth considering: salt makes a person thirsty.

Do we Christians make people thirsty for the Water of Life?

#2 · · · · A Bible Study During Tough Times

Nothing can touch a child of God without His permission. (Read Job 1 and 2.)

God is sovereign.

> II Chronicles 20:6
> Isaiah 40
> Isaiah 43
> I Chronicles 29:10–14
> Lamentations 3:37
>
> (And many others. As you
> read through the Bible, note this.)

"There is no wisdom nor understanding nor counsel against the Lord."

—PROVERBS 21:30

or

"Intelligence, skill, strategy—none can avail against the Eternal."
—PROVERBS 21:30, MOFFATT

SO . . .

For the child of God, are there any secondary causes? Satan must get God's permission before he can touch Job's possessions, much less Job. So when Job lost everything, he worshipped and said: *The Lord gave and the Lord* [not Satan] *hath taken away; blessed be the name of the Lord."*

Shimei cursed the fleeing King David and when David's

men wanted to kill Shimei, David said no, *"God hath bidden him curse"* (II SAMUEL 16:11).

Our Lord said to Pilate (when Pilate said, *"Knowest Thou not that I have power to crucify Thee, and have power to release Thee?"*), *"Thou couldst have no power at all against me, except it were given thee from above"* (JOHN 19:10–11).

Later Paul, in a Roman prison, writes: *"Be not thou therefore ashamed of the testimony of our Lord, nor of me His prisoner* [not prisoner of Rome, but of God]*"* (II TIMOTHY 1:8).

SO . . .

• • • • • ∽⊃◯ • • • • •

"The fool hath said in his heart, There is no God" (PSALM 14:1).

This goes also for those who doubt His sovereignty. Either He is sovereign or He is not. If He is not sovereign He is not God. Therefore when we become so preoccupied with and dismayed by circumstances and certain people that we doubt God's ability to handle them in His own way, and in His own time, then we, too, are fools.

• • • • • ∽⊃◯ • • • • •

It is this knowledge that enables us to accept the unacceptable. We can take whatever comes as from His hand, submit to it, and learn of Him all He seeks to teach us through those circumstances.

Read   Genesis 16:9
        Luke 2:51
        James 4:6–8a

Learn of Him. Matthew 11:29.

"It was our Lord's meekness and lowliness that made His great burden so light . . . And it is out of His own experience that He speaks to us. 'Bring but a meek heart to your burden as I did,' He says to us. 'Bring but the same mind to your yoke as I brought to My yoke, and see how easy it will feel,' . . . Go to Him in any case, and whatever He sees it good to do with you and your burden, He will at any rate begin to give you another heart under it. He will begin to give you a meek and lowly heart. . . . It is not your burden that weighs you down. It is your proud, rebellious self-seeking, self-pleasing heart. . . . Had He dealt with you after your sins and rewarded you according to your iniquities, you would not have been here to find fault with the way He is leading you to pardon, peace and everlasting life."
—ALEXANDER WHYTE

Second Corinthians 6:4. *"In all things approving ourselves . . . in much patience, in afflictions, in necessities, in distresses."*

"Patience in Greek means literally endurance. *It is more than patient submissiveness. There is a note of triumph. It is the ability to bear things in such a triumphant way that it transfigures them. It enables a man to pass the breaking point and not to break, and always to greet the unseen with a cheer.*

"Afflictions in Greek means pressure. *The things which press sore upon us. Originally it expressed sheer physical pressure on a man. . . . The sheer pressure of the demands of life upon one."*
—WILLIAM BARCLAY

God's grace is not only sufficient—it is inexhaustible. Remember the story Roy Gustafson told of the little fish who said, *"I am so thirsty but I must not drink too much. The ocean might run dry."* Or the little mouse in the granaries of Egypt who said,

"I am so hungry. But I must not eat too much. The grain might not last." Or the little swallow, soaring and dipping through the sky, thinking, *"I must not breathe too deeply; I might use up all the air."*

Whatever the need, whatever the situation, *"he giveth more grace"* (JAMES 4:6).

・・・・・ ⌇⌇⌇ ・・・・・

Delight———Submit———Learn———Shift goals———
Worship———Take all He has to offer.

Delight	Psalm 37:4 (Read all of Psalm 37. List the commands. Do them.)
Submit	Genesis 16:9 Luke 2:51 James 4:6–8a (No secondary causes)
Learn His lessons	Psalm 25:4–5 Psalm 27:11 Matthew 11:29

Be God's eager pupil.
Dan Piatt (who lost three members of his family in one car accident) said after the tragedy: *"I told God that I wanted to learn everything He had to teach me through this experience."*
The Matthews on their house arrest in the Orient: *"We stopped looking for a way to escape and began instead to ask God to teach us all He had for us to learn from this experience."*

Shift goals—from personal happiness to His glory.
"Man's chief end is" not personal happiness, but *"to glorify God and to enjoy Him forever."*

Read John 12:24–28. Pray not, *"Father, save me"*—but *"Father, glorify Thy name."*

Worship—when you cannot understand.

Job—when word came that he had lost everything—*"fell down upon the ground, and worshiped"* (JOB 1:20).

Hannah—after leaving the newly weaned Samuel with Eli in the temple—*"worshiped"* (I SAMUEL 1:28; 2:1).

David—fleeing from Absalom, when he reached the top of the Mount of Olives, *"worshiped"* (II SAMUEL 15:32).

When he heard that his child by Bathsheba was dead—*"worshiped"* (II SAMUEL 12:20).

43 · · · · Motivation

"There are no lazy kids," someone observed, *"only unmotivated
ones."*

The same goes for adults.

· · · · · ∽⟨⟩ · · · · ·

Suddenly the grandfather of the tribe decided to go
swimming. The ladder was lowered, and he and son-in-law
Stephan started down. The grandfather, lithe and trim as a
thirty-year-old, moving slowly and stiffly as a ninety-year-old,

"I'm getting old," he said as he looked carefully where next
to put his foot.

". . . just fourteen years from eighty . . . harder to move, all
the time . . . I'm getting so stiff . . ." And rung by difficult rung
he slowly lowered himself into the delicious water. Here, he and
Stephan swam and floated around leisurely and blissfully.

I was watching from the upper deck with our daughter, Gigi,
who was expecting our sixteenth grandchild in two weeks.

Suddenly off to their left, deep in the clear water, appeared
a long, thin, unmistakable shadow, moving swiftly toward the
swimmers.

"Bill!" I shouted. "There's a barracuda!"

Zip! He was up that ladder in nothing flat. He lost fifty years
in one second!

······ ⌇⌇ ······

I thought of the toad in the deep rut when the little rabbit hopped by.

"Hey!" called the rabbit. "What are you doing down there?"

"Can't get out," said the toad.

Later when the rabbit returned, he met the toad face-to-face on the side of the road.

"Hey, I thought you couldn't get out?" said the rabbit.

"I couldn't," toad replied, "but along came a truck, and I had to."

····· ⌇⌇ ·····

And so it is with me often: unexpected danger, an impossible situation, will be used by God to make things happen.

The handful of believers commissioned by Jesus to go into all the world and preach the Gospel met daily in the Temple (whose very leaders had urged the Romans to crucify their Lord), worshipping and praising God. Then came the stunning fact that Stephen, one of their leaders, had been stoned to death. Persecution had begun. And with it, the beginning of the fulfillment of the Great Commission. The persecutor, himself arrested by God, became Paul the persecuted, leading the way in carrying the Gospel to the stronghold of Caesar himself.

So by unexpected means God frequently makes possible the impossible—motivating the unmotivated.

Had any ideas lately?

44 ···· "He Makes It Taste Like Tea"

In one of F. W. Boreham's books, he tells of an old Scottish woman living alone and very poor.

But she carefully tithed what little she had and gave to the church. When unable to attend service, she expected a deacon to drop by and collect her offering. The deacon knew well she could not afford it, but knowing also that she would be deeply offended if he did not collect it, he was careful to stop by.

It was late afternoon one day when he made his visit.

Old Mary was sitting near a window having tea.

"The tithe is on the mantel," she said, greetings over. *"Won't ye sit and have a cup of tea?"*

The deacon sat, and when Mary passed him his cup, he looked down in surprise and exclaimed:

"Why, Mary! It's only water ye have!"

"Aye!" said old Mary. *"But He makes it taste like tea!"*

45···· Enlarge My Heart

Enlarge my heart
to love You more,
when I am stumbling
on the way;
only the heart
enlarged by You,
runs to obey.

Psalm 119:32

46 · · · · Outwitted

Bill and Grady Wilson had left for Moscow in 1959, leaving Wilma and me under the watchful eye of an old college friend living in Paris, Jeanette Evans.

"Now don't go shopping," were Bill's final words.

We waited for the plane to disappear out of sight and headed for the nearest junk shop.

With Jeanette's expert French we managed beautifully. Wilma found several irresistibles: an epergne, a silver inkwell adorned with cupids, and one or two more things.

I found one lovely little painting I couldn't resist—price, translated from French currency to American, came to ten dollars—and a piece of needlepoint, not particularly pretty, but dirt cheap. It was enough to cover a footstool. I handled lovingly and longingly some blue-and-white primitive plates with peasant scenes on them, but, considering the weight, my conscience getting the best of me, I turned them down. (They were about fifty cents each.)

So the shopkeeper accepted our francs and wrapped our purchases carefully for carrying—in two packages.

Then we began figuring. Wilma's package was larger than mine.

"Let me carry yours and you can carry mine," I suggested. "I can explain to Bill that it's something you bought. And should Grady notice that you're carrying something, you can explain it's mine."

But at the hotel that night in Versailles we couldn't resist unwrapping our treasures.

I propped my painting on the mantel over the fireplace and admired it.

Wilma placed her acquisitions on the desk, likewise enjoying her lovely old French bargains.

When our husbands returned from Moscow, they drove to Versailles to pick us up. We were to begin driving to Zurich, Switzerland, that afternoon.

Wilma and I were packing when Grady came in to hurry us up.

"I like this picture so much," I said on an impulse, "I just think I'll take it with me." And taking my painting from the mantel, I packed it in my suitcase.

Catching on, Wilma exclaimed, "And I like this inkwell so much I think I'll just take *it*." Whereupon she picked up her cupid-decorated inkstand and, fitting it in her case, closed it.

Miles on our way I got to thinking about what we had done and started to laugh.

"What's so funny?" Grady wanted to know.

So, laughing, we told him about our trip to the junk (not antique) shop, our purchases, and what we had done at the hotel.

Silence.

"What's wrong?" I asked. "We spent practically nothing."

"Well," Grady said, "it's just that when Wilma's back was turned, I took the inkwell out and put it back on the desk."

#7 · · · · God Has No Answering Service

First I called Northwest Airlines. A man's voice came on, saying, "Due to heavy traffic, we are unable to help you at this time. If you will kindly wait, someone will be with you shortly."

Next I called Eastern. After listening to repeated ringing, I heard a female voice begin:

"Thank you for calling Eastern. Due to the increase in calls, there will be a slight delay in answering. To assist us in answering your question, would you be prepared to give us the following information—your destination, number in party, including children . . . ," etc., etc.

I turned to Delta only to receive the same noncommittal answering service.

So, I started all over. Each time the same response. One time I even got the wrong number and who do you suppose answered? You guessed it. An answering service.

It was Saturday, and offices were closed. I called our home office which usually has a weekend operator on the switchboard. But I got—an answering service!

Frustrated, I tried to call my husband who happened to be in Nova Scotia and got one of my husband's associates who, while not being as satisfactory as one's husband, is certainly better than an answering service. He put me in touch with a local travel agent who suggested I call him back on his WATS line. I did, and the problem was eventually solved.

How grateful we can be that God has no answering service.

"In my distress I called upon the Lord, and cried unto my God: he heard my voice . . . and my cry came before him, even in to his ears."

—PSALM 18:6

"And it shall come to pass, that before they call, I will answer; and while they are yet speaking, I will hear."

—ISAIAH 65:24

48 · · · · They Come and Go So Quickly

They come and go so quickly
Spring and Fall . . .
as if they had not really
come at all.
Perhaps
we could not take
too much of beauty,
breath-catching glory,
ecstasy without relief;
and so
God made them
brief.

49 · · · · Hands Larger than Ours

On my way to China in 1980, I stopped to visit friends in California. The American grandmother had spent fifty-three years in China where her Chinese husband had died during the Cultural Revolution (1966–76). Her three children, all born there, were now here with her, but her two grandchildren were still in Peking. They had their government's permission to leave, but were waiting for our State Department to process their visas.

The day I visited was the grandmother's eighty-eighth birthday. And I wanted to get pictures of her and the family to take to the two still in Peking.

Thinking how nice it would be to surprise her with their arrival on her birthday, I had called the proper authorities to see what could be done. They said they would try.

But her birthday arrived without her grandchildren. I felt free to tell them at least we had tried.

The pretty young mother, in her charming broken English, said, "I would like to tell you a story.

"Once there was a kind seller of cherries. A small boy was watching him. The small boy loved cherries, but he had no money to buy with, only his eyes.

"And the kind seller of cherries saw the small boy and asked,

" 'You want some cherries?'

"The small boy nodded his head.

" 'Hold out your hands,' said the kind seller of cherries.

"But the small boy would not.

" 'Hold out your hands,' repeated the seller of the cherries.

"Still the small boy did not move.

95

"So the kind seller of cherries gathered both his hands full of cherries and told the small boy to hold out his shirt, filling it with cherries.

"When he got home, his grandmother asked,

"'Why did you not hold out your hands when the kind seller of cherries told you to?'

"'Because,' the small boy said, 'his hands were bigger than mine.'

"His hands are bigger than ours." And the young mother smiled. "We can wait."

50 · · · · Prospering in Sin

"*To prosper in sin,*" wrote John Trapp in seventeenth-century England, "*is the greatest tragedy that can befall a man this side of hell.*"

When we pray earnestly for a beloved prodigal and calamity falls, we must be lovingly sympathetic—but thank God that He is working. Trouble is just the old sheepdog nudging us back to the Shepherd.

The psalmist marvels at the wicked "*spreading himself like a green bay tree.*" The Prayer Book version puts it: "*like a green native plant.*" We have a schefflera plant in our living room. It makes a nice houseplant where we live because it is not a native plant. But a schefflera plant in Florida grows to be a tree.

Why should we wonder, then, when we Christians struggle? We are not native plants. This earth is not our home, and we can expect to have rough times. Our Lord promised us that.

So John Trapp looked around him at the prosperous ungodly of his day and wrote, in his inimitable way, "*Envy not such an one his pomp any more than you would a corpse his flowers.*"

51 · · · · · Ever New Beginnings

They splashed and they flopped, those aspiring wind surfers. Day after day we chronicled their struggles. It looked simple enough: a surfboard, a detachable sail with a length of rope tied to it, water, wind and, of course, instruction.

But how they flopped! First the sail would go flat in the water, with the surfer going splash under the water on the other side, or making a quick jump to avoid being clobbered by the mast. Then would come the struggle to get aboard again, the balancing act, the careful pulling of the sail back to position— then plop! It all had to be done over again.

The following summer we discovered a few surfers who had more or less mastered the art. They skimmed about with surprising skill even on rough days. One had so much confidence that he even sailed with his jacket on, maneuvering his craft skillfully wherever he wished it to go. He was so cocky. I kept hoping he would flop just once, but he had learned well.

He was, we discovered, the instructor.

We watched surfers go to the aid of a fallen surfer, heard them shouting encouragement to one another. And when the instructor spoke, they listened, and tried carefully to do what he said. Wind surfing is a challenge, a skill to be mastered. It is a practice in unending patience and dogged determination.

Like wind surfing, the Christian life is simple but not easy. And we are not born into God's family fully grown, although at times we treat baby Christians as if they should have been.

We who are older in the Christian walk and those who, through experience, have earned the status of instructor should be quick to encourage, quick to help the one who has fallen.

We who have not yet mastered the art of Christian living

need to keep carefully studying our Book of Instructions, listening attentively when our Instructor speaks, and promptly following His instructions.

Alexander Whyte of Edinburgh once said: *"The perseverance of the saints consists in ever new beginnings."*

· · · · · ✑∽◯ · · · · ·

In 1962 Sir Francis Chichester sailed the Atlantic in 33 days, lopping one week off his 1960 record but failing to reach his target of 30 days. Of this failure he said, "If I had succeeded, I should have been deprived of the immense sport, anticipation, hope and excitement of trying again."
—LONDON, Sunday Times Magazine
MAY 7, 1967

· · · · · ✑∽◯ · · · · ·

"How did you learn to skate?" someone asked the winner. *"By getting up every time I fell down,"* was the reply.

52····Ignored

Our daughter was visiting with Velma Barfield in the women's prison in Raleigh, shortly before her execution.

Each prisoner had her own little cubicle for visiting with friends or family members even while being separated by a partition and having to visit through a pane of glass. There was a window in the door through which the guard could see everything.

For Anne and Velma, the little cubicle was touched with glory, for there were not two but three there. And the reality of Jesus' presence, and the nearness of Heaven awaiting Velma, gave special meaning to the visit.

When the time was up, the guard simply opened all the doors.

As Anne left, she turned to wave to Velma.

It was then she realized with horror that there were prisoners sitting in their little cubicles behind their glass partitions whom no one had bothered to visit.

53 ···· God Bless and Fortify Them

"God bless and fortify them,
God hear when they entreat,
The strong courageous people
Too brave to own defeat.

"And oh, God, bless and help them,
God answer when they call,
The tired defeated people
Who are not brave at all."
                    —JANE MERCHANT

54····Giving God Pleasure

Grandmother's brother, Uncle Eddie McCue, lived on the old pre-Civil War home place, "Belvidere," in the Shenandoah Valley of Virginia.

One day, while working the farm, he discarded his coat and told his collie dog, Chunk, to watch it.

That night, when Uncle Eddie got back to the house, he missed Chunk. No one had seen him. They called, but there was no response. Distressed, they ate supper, then continued searching. Bedtime came and still no Chunk. The next morning they looked outside hopefully. No sign of the old collie.

Time came for Uncle Eddie to return to the fields to work. There, in a distant field he saw something lying on the ground— his forgotten coat. And beside it lay Chunk, head and ears up, his plumed tail thumping the ground in the eager welcome.

That was years ago.

Tonight, as I sit on the porch, our old German shepherd is lying at my feet. He lifts his great head as a low mutter of thunder rumbles in the distance, and gives a deep warning bark. Then as the storm nears, he rises with a lurch and tears into the front yard to meet it. The yard is a brief ledge confined by an old rail fence, beyond which it falls precipitously down a bank and is engulfed by the encroaching woods.

The storm is on us, the great dog furiously doing battle with it. As it passes, he returns to the porch, settling contentedly at my feet convinced he has driven it away.

Protecting and pleasing us is his very life.

He is a German guard dog, given to us years ago by concerned friends. He had been carefully trained in search and rescue, attack, and obedience.

Search and rescue in these mountains can come in handy. Previous dogs of ours had been used successfully for that purpose.

I cannot imagine an occasion when we would give the order to attack. But a well-trained dog can sense hostility or spot a weapon (or even what resembles a weapon) in which case it's a wise person who freezes in his tracks.

But it's the obedience training that gives us real joy. To stop, to sit, to lie down, to go away, to search, to stay, to heel. A disobedient dog is not only a headache; he can be a liability. Obedience makes a dog a joy.

Is it less so with God and His children?

There are some I know who have been trained in attack. We will not mention names. You may know a few. But they are skilled at it.

Then there are those trained in search and rescue. (I'd put the Salvation Army in this group.)

And there are those who have been trained in obedience.

I think this, more than anything else, must give the Lord pleasure. Simple obedience. Joyful, eager, unquestioning obedience; to be able to say with the psalmist, "I *delight to do thy will, O my God,*" would be the height of training for the Christian.

For it is this that gives God the greatest pleasure.

55 · · · · "Hurry Up, Mom!"

Ned was not quite tall enough to see over the dashboard of the car I was driving.

"Hurry up, Mom!" he urged.

But he was too young to read the road signs that said 45 miles per hour. As I began to apply the brakes, he demanded, "Why are you stopping?"

"There's a school bus that has just stopped," I explained.

As soon as we started again, he urged, "Pass him, Mom." He was too small to see the double yellow line.

I thought to myself, How like me when I pray! Spiritually I am too young to read the road signs, too small to see what lies ahead. Yet how often I am guilty of telling God how to run things.

We may make requests, but never insist on having our own way lest we become one of those of whom it was said, *"He gave them their request; but sent leanness into their soul"* (PSALM 106:15).

We may pray in simple, childlike faith; urgently, persistently. But we must always pray, "Thy will be done."

56 · · · · Small Prayers

". . . and please pray I'll catch a lizard."

Alone in the kitchen, catching up on the mail, I came across this very serious request to *The Samaritan's Purse* from a very serious four-year-old supporter.

I laughed aloud. I loved it!

I thought of Murdock, the giant gray lizard who inhabits the old hewn logs outside the bay window of our bedroom, and of Matilda, his somewhat smaller wife.

"A baby lizard," I wrote one October morning, "crawled up the topmost log of those stacked beneath the bedroom window and stared solemnly at me. I stared back, not quite so solemnly. Soon he scrambled off.

"But that brief, lighthearted moment brightened my day."

So I, too, am an appreciator of lizards.

Only the day before I read this four-year-old's prayer request, we had been in Paris where I had been with Bill for Mission France. Much prayer had gone up all over France in behalf of those who might be unfulfilled spiritually and stifled materially.

And here was a small boy praying for a lizard!

And God, our Father, who so graciously answered prayer in France, cared also for the concern of one small four-year-old.

I wondered how God not only puts up with, but welcomes our prayers, considering *all* He has on Him.

Not once has He ever said, "Don't bother Me. Don't you see I'm busy?" And He so well could—with a world in its present condition.

No. Each person is special to Him, Who calls every star by name, Who has the hairs of our heads numbered, and Who knows the number of grains of sand on the ocean shores.

So even a small boy's desire for a lizard would be duly noted. In fact, I imagine the angels themselves enjoyed that small request—with, perhaps, angelic chuckles.

• • • • • ⌒⌒⌒⌒ • • • • •

I remembered a little poem which Amy Carmichael found in a magazine and quoted. So I looked it up.

> "And then a little laughing prayer
>   Came running up the sky,
> Above the golden gutters, where
>   The sorry prayers go by.
> It had no fear of anything,
>   But in that holy place
> It found the very throne of God
>   And smiled up in His face."

57 · · · · Ashamed to Repent

"God cannot forgive excuses; He can only forgive sins."
—CALVIN THIELMAN

· · · · · ⧢ · · · · ·

"The Christian must be consumed with the infinite beauty of holiness and the infinite damnability of sin."
—THOMAS CARLYLE

· · · · · ⧢ · · · · ·

"A noble mind disdains not to repent."
—HOMER
Iliad, Book 15, Line 157

· · · · · ⧢ · · · · ·

"How irrational human nature is, especially that of youth. They are not ashamed to sin and yet they are ashamed to repent. They are ashamed of the very returning which alone can make them to be truly wise men."
—DANIEL DEFOE
in the original Robinson Crusoe

"You mean I have to go to the front when Billy gives an invitation?"

"Yes."

"But," he objected, "everybody will see me."

I pictured the fifteen thousand in the Madison Square Garden and wondered who would notice one small Puerto Rican teenager.

"You weren't embarrassed to steal, to cheat, to lie," I said to him. "Now you're ashamed to take a public stand for Jesus? Nuts!"

58 · · · · A Young Rebel

The young rebel was just one among the crowd of students that night in the Knoxville stadium, demonstrating against the meetings. He disliked Billy Graham immensely and understandably as, since a small boy, he was made to watch Bill whenever he was on TV.

He had heard the old invitation before . . . "hundreds of you will be coming forward to make your commitment to Christ . . ." And he knew it was just a gimmick.

Toward the end of the message, the young rebel felt Bill was speaking, not to the packed stadium, but directly to him, personally.

Then came the invitation. "Hundreds of you will be coming forward to receive Christ . . ." And suddenly they were. From every corner of the stadium, quietly, reverently . . .

The young rebel turned and left the stadium quickly.

But the next night he was back, and when the invitation was given, he was among those who went forward and gave his life to Christ.

He went on to college and majored in Bible and minored in art (as I had). Today we have the pleasure of him working in our organization.   • • • • • ⌒⌒⌒ • • • • •

Perhaps another coincidence. In 1954, a small boy from Wales attended the meetings at Harringay Arena, in the north of London.

He was only fifteen, but a caring teacher had collected him and a group of schoolmates, and together they had gone to hear this "bloke Bill Graem." That night the Lord found that fifteen-year-old. He grew up and went to Vietnam as a missionary. There he met and married a fellow missionary, an American, nicknamed Dixie. When Vietnam closed, he settled in America, got his Ph.D. somewhere along the line, and eventually entered Christian book publishing.

He's Victor Oliver of Oliver-Nelson, publisher of this book.

59 · · · · Traveling Light

"I'd like to see you gain a few pounds," I said to our tall, lanky son, Ned.

"No way," he replied. "It would be just that much more to haul up the rock." Rock climbing had become his latest enthusiasm.

I watched him chin himself, using only his fingertips curled over the top of the kitchen door frame. Then he repeated the process, using only one arm. Finger grips are important in rock climbing and so is keeping in shape. And I was learning as I listened and watched.

The Christian life is a climb. For some, it is a gently sloping ascent; for others, it is more like attacking the north face of the Eiger.

Christina Rossetti wrote:

> "Does the road climb uphill all the way?
> Yes, to the very end.
> Does the day's journey take the whole day long?
> From morn to night, my friend."

For Christians, keeping in shape spiritually and traveling light are important. To keep in shape spiritually, we need spiritual nourishment and exercise. We need to read about the Bible less and to actually read and study it more. Then we need to carefully and vigorously apply it to our daily lives, to live out what we have taken in.

The definition of traveling light may vary from one individual to another. For example, I couldn't get my work done if I had to carry around a rock climber's backpack loaded with rock-climbing gear. But most of us need to trim off some excess weight. We have too many social involvements, an overabundance of good but unnecessary meetings. We are on more boards than one person can adequately or usefully serve. Remember the caution: *"Beware of the barrenness of a busy life."*

Young David refused Saul's armor when he confronted Goliath (I SAMUEL 17:39–40).

Gideon had to trim down the size of his army (JUDGES 7).

The disciples really traveled light when they were sent out two by two, *"without purse, and scrip, and shoes"* (LUKE 22:35).

Situations vary, times change, and God's orders to His followers are individualized. It is only the need and the message that continue the same—and the goal.

It is up to us to keep in shape and travel light.

60 ···· Clogged Pens

I shook it. I knocked it gently, sideways on the top of the desk. I licked a piece of paper and wrote carefully in the moisture (I can't tell you why this works, but it usually does). I repeated each procedure without results. Then I carried the pen to the sink, took it apart, and carefully flushed out the point. Refilling it, I sat down to write.

How like me, I thought with exasperation.

I have mugs full of pens on my desk: ballpoints, felt tips, ink pens—even pencils. But for very fine writing, such as notes in the margin of my Bible, I need a Rapidograph pen. This pen has a needle-fine point and uses India ink, which will not seep through or smear on the thin India paper.

How often when God has needed me I have been clogged up (too busy or inundated with things—the necessary giving way to the unnecessary). Or I've gone dry.

When that happens, I need a "shaking up," or I need special cleansing. And I need to be filled and refilled and filled again.

There have been times when God has patiently and carefully done just that. There have been other times when He has had to pass me over and pick up a pen that was usable.

But unlike a pen, I do have a choice. I can decide whether or not I remain usable.

61·····The Land Rover

"Mom," Franklin said one day. "The sanitorium at Mafraq sure does need a Land Rover."

Number one son had for several summers worked with a travel agency under tour director Roy Gustafson as tour escort. On each tour they visited the Annor Tubercular Sanitorium at Mafraq, Jordan.

At that point I wasn't sure what a Land Rover was—a form of security or a special kind of dog. I learned fast.

"The Jordanian army up and took theirs, no permission nor nothin'."

"Why?"

"There was a war going on, and they needed it. Now the hospital has no way of getting around. And being fifty miles out in the desert from Amman, that's tough."

"Where does one get a Land Rover?" I asked.

"Oh yes," he added, "it has to be fully equipped for the desert. In London, I guess," answering my question.

"Okay. I'll talk to Dad about it."

After Bill got home and understood the situation, he agreed something had to be done. And true to form, he wasted no time.

Jean Wilson, who had worked with us in England for years, was contacted.

Would she locate a Land Rover, fully equipped for the desert, and have it ready by the following Monday morning?

She would.

Franklin had already convinced us he should pick it up and drive it to Jordan.

We felt, at this point, the experience would do more for him than a semester at college, in which he was less than interested.

But for obvious reasons he needed an able companion. We thought of Bill Cristobal, his college roommate.

Bill had become a Christian after he was grown. After which he had had three tours of duty in Vietnam as a helicopter pilot, spending his R & R's visiting and helping out missionaries in Southeast Asia. Bill is solid, sensible, loving the Lord his God with all his *"heart, soul, mind and strength,"* and his neighbor as himself. Bill is not only a highly qualified helicopter pilot and a committed Christian, he radiates a quiet confidence and joy in life that explodes frequently into contagious laughter.

Later he volunteered to fly for Wycliffe Bible Translators, but before he would accept his first assignment, he took time off to build his aging mother an adequate, comfortable house, using his Vietnam savings. That's Bill.

So we asked Bill if he would consider dropping out of school one semester and going with Franklin on this trip. He agreed.

Bill knew Franklin. He knew he was a spiritual goof-off, but the two liked and enjoyed one another, and Franklin had great respect for Bill's character as well as his ability.

· · · · · ⌒⌒ · · · · ·

In London, Jean Wilson headed for the Land Rover dealership.

Now Jean is tall—almost six feet—ample, with a cheerful self-confidence, and a keen mind.

As she loomed through the door of the salesroom, she returned the salesman's very proper greeting with overwhelming good cheer. Wasting no more time than necessary on useless pleasantries, she got right down to business. She would like, if you please, a Land Rover, fully-equipped-for-the-desert, and would pick it up Monday morning.

The salesman looked at her in disbelief.

"But, madam . . . ," he replied with dignity.

"One does not simply ask for a Land Rover fully equipped for the desert and expect to pick it up on such short notice. One places one's order, and after a year, one picks . . ."

114

"I know, I know," Jean interrupted cheerily but firmly. "But I happen to need one by this coming Monday morning."

"Madam," the salesman tried to make himself look a little taller and sound much more firm. "You do not understand. One does not simply pick up a Land Rover like that. One places one's order and . . ."

"I know. I know. I heard you the first time," interrupted the intrepid Jean. "But would you mind going to the warehouse and just looking about to see if you should just happen to have a Land Rover fully-equipped-for-the-desert in stock?"

"Yes, madam," said the salesman with considerable restraint.

Turning on his heel, he disappeared through the door.

After some time he returned, somewhat bewildered and incredulous.

"Madam," he stammered, "I, I do not understand—it was most unlikely, unthinkable—but I find we do happen to have a Land Rover in the warehouse, fully equipped for the desert." Adding, as he sat down abruptly,

"And you may pick it up on Monday!"

62 ···· John 17 and Me

As I thought of Franklin and Bill Cristobal picking up the
Land Rover in London that Monday evening, driving it on the
left-hand side of the road till they arrived at Dover, then driving
it across France, Switzerland, Austria, Yugoslavia, Greece, Turkey,
Syria, Lebanon, back into Syria, and down into Jordan, this
mother's heart sank.

Unable to concentrate, I finally got my Bible and turned to
John 17, our Lord's prayer for His disciples before His crucifixion.

I needed to pray for our son and his buddy—somehow I felt
this prayer would fit.

Suddenly verse 19 brought me up short.

Remember, it was our Lord Himself praying.

"For their sakes," Jesus prayed, *"I sanctify myself that they also
may be truly consecrated through the truth . . ."* (Sanctify means to
set apart, to commit, to consecrate.)

This was our Lord Himself praying.

I could not miss it. I could not bypass it. I had to handle it
head-on.

For Franklin and Bill Cristobal's sake, I needed to recommit
my life to God before I could ask that He do that for them.

I prayed, "Lord, You take care of them. I need to settle some
things in my own life with You."

It is unrealistic to ask the Lord to do in someone else's life
that which we are unwilling for Him to do in ours.

So, putting Bill and Franklin "on hold," I settled some
things with God that day.

The load lifted and peace came.

63 · · · · "Have I Been a Wilderness . . . ?"

"Have I been a wilderness to You?"
        asked the Lord.
"A place of wandering
and of darkness
        as the night?"

No—
It is this void
in which I find myself.
This is my wilderness,
my place of wandering
in darkness and in fog.
You are light
and life.
All I long for,
all I need,
is You.
How can we walk together
once again?
How can I know You, Lord,
as once I knew?
And He
through the echoing of my empty heart
replied,
"I shall be waiting for you
at the very spot
you left My side."

64 · · · · Delivered

The Land Rover eventually and eventfully delivered to
Mafraq, Franklin and Bill stayed on to help wherever they could,
mainly in construction, sharing the rooftop at night, sleeping
beneath the stars, brilliant in the desert sky. In bad weather,
Franklin moved to the garage with a fellow worker—an Arab
named Mohammed.

Here Mohammed patiently taught Franklin Arabic words and
phrases night after night till they fell asleep.

And as he worked, he silently observed Dr. Eleanor Soltau
and head nurse, Aileen Coleman.

Both women were fearless six-footers in a land run by males.
Both had medical skills, no-nonsense Christian commitment,
unlimited compassion, and the ability to enjoy life to the fullest.
Both were equally unaware of the deep, lasting impression their
lives were having on one American teenager who watched them
as he worked.

And who grew up eventually to become Chairman of the
Board of the Annor Tubercular Sanitorium in Mafraq, Jordan.

65 ···· Enemies?

It was the year 1937.

The freight car stood all day beneath a row of trees in China to protect them from enemy planes. It was filled with missionaries feeling the approaching Japanese army. The Chinese landscape was bleak, the heat oppressive.

A lone Japanese guard walked the platform—back and forth, back and forth—eyeing the occupants each time he passed.

His face was inscrutable. The staccato comments to a few nearby soldiers sounded threatening. The missionaries prayed silently, expecting the worst, praying for darkness so they could move on.

Darkness came, and as the train began to move, the guard approached and quickly handed his folding fan to one of the missionaries.

As the train picked up speed, the missionary gratefully unfolded the fan to find relief from the unrelenting heat. Inside the fan was written:

"God bless you. I too Christian."

· · · · · ~⌒~ · · · · ·

Sam Moffett (former missionary to Korea, now Professor Emeritus of Ecumenics and Mission at Princeton Theological Seminary) tells of a man in the U.S. Diplomatic Corps at Panmunjom. He was there to help work out a peaceful solution—or at least to maintain what peace there was.

One night, discouraged and tired, he headed toward his sleeping quarters. As he walked, he whistled "What a friend we have in Jesus . . ."

Suddenly he heard something.

He stopped—and listened.

Across the black expanse that was no-man's-land, he heard a responding whistle, "What a friend we have in Jesus . . ."

Somewhere on the enemy side was a fellow believer.

66····God's Ways Seem Dark

"God's ways seem dark,
but soon or late,
They touch the shining
hills of day."
                    —J. G. WHITTIER

· · · · · ⚬ · · · · ·

"If peace be in the heart
The wildest winter storm is full of solemn beauty . . ."
                    —C. F. RICHARDSON

67···Three Cheers for Incompatibility!

Last month, another well-known couple terminated a long and apparently agreeable marriage. The reason given: incompatibility—an all-too-familiar legal umbrella under which an assortment of excuses can find shelter.

I looked up the dictionary definition of *incompatibility* and brushed it aside as beside the point: *"incapable of coexisting harmoniously, discordant, mismated . . ."*

"Incapable of coexisting harmoniously"? *"With God all things are possible."*

My husband was given a Swiss watch by our daughter Gigi's Swiss in-laws. When it stopped, no local watchmaker could fix it. The next time we were in Switzerland we sent it directly to the people who had made it. They had no problem; the ones who made it knew how to make it work again.

Who invented marriage? He is the One to whom we must go. His Book of Instructions has the answers.

"Disagreeing in nature . . ." Great! One can disagree without being disagreeable. Before we were married, someone gave me a gem of wisdom: *"Where two people agree on everything, one of them is unnecessary."*

"Irreconcilable . . ." I doubt it! When two draw near to God, they find themselves closer to one another.

"Conflicting . . ." Terrific! I once knew a man who refused to let his wife disagree with him on anything. Now, every man *needs* to be disagreed with occasionally. This poor man's personality, his ego, and even his judgment suffered.

When someone gets into a position of political or social power or one of fame or fortune and no one dares to disagree with him, look out! He is in danger. At times, we *all* need to be disagreed with.

Pat Scott, Mamie Eisenhower and I were lunching one day while our husbands relaxed over what for me would have been hard work: a game of golf.

"Would you two like to know the secret of our happy marriage?" our older companion asked.

Forks in midair, we waited.

"Because," and the mischievous eyes brimmed with laughter, "we never do anything together."

"Except," she added with an irrepressible laugh, "sleep together."

We were still laughing when our husbands joined us. Her words ringing in my ears, I noticed the affectionate kiss with which her husband greeted her, his loving hand on her shoulder.

All I can say is, "Three cheers for incompatibility!"

68····Leave Them to God

Leave them to God
those distant, sinister souls
whose crimes unmentionable
stained history's pages red,
decimated races,
searing the minds of survivors;
leave them to God.
For there are those today
perpetrating crimes
as hideous as theirs;
unnoticed and unmentioned.
Only the past concerns.
What if in satisfying vengeance
we sacrifice the living for the dead?
divert attention from the present
        holocaust?
Why must more die
while those who could help
dwell in mental ghettos
of a time now gone?
Perhaps some evil force
would have it so.
And still they die.
Diversionary tactics?
Is that why?

69 · · · · "He Shall Become My Son"

During a heated argument, one young Bedouin struck and killed another.

Bedouin is the Aramaic name for "desert dwellers."

The people, little known to the Western world, are rich in tradition and custom, much of it closely aligned with Biblical teachings.

These nomads are descendants of Abraham and Sarah's Egyptian handmaid, Hagar, and refer to *"our great father, Abraham."*

Their mode of living closely resembles that of their father Abraham who also lived in goat-hair tents, traveling from place to place in the desert.

The Arab temper, like that of many other cultures, has a low boiling point. Usually it explodes in earsplitting curses and the flailing of arms.

But the young man had killed his friend, now lying dead in the sand, the victim of second-degree murder.

Knowing the ancient, inflexible custom of his people, he fled, running across the desert under cover of darkness, till he came to the sprawling black tent of the tribal chief.

Confessing his crime, he asked for protection and, according to Old Testament law, was granted asylum.

The old chief put his hand on one of the guy-ropes of the great tent, swore by Allah, and took the young Arab under his protection—until the affair could be settled legally.

The next day, the young man's pursuers arrived, demanding the murderer be turned over to them.

"But I have given my word," the old chieftain said.

"But you don't know who he killed!" they said.

"I have given my word."

"He killed *your son!*"

The old chieftain was visibly shaken. He stood, head bowed, for quite some time, as the accused and the accusers as well as the curious onlookers waited breathlessly.

Finally the old man raised his head. He stood upright.

"Then he shall become my son," he said, "and everything I have will one day be his."

(Told to me by Roy Gustafson)

70 · · · · Scaffolding

The famous Tienanmen (Gate of Heavenly Peace) in Beijing, China, was shrouded in bamboo scaffolding. The impressive structure, originally erected during the reign of Emperor Yung Lo in 1417, was restored in 1651. But the old gate was showing the wear of time, the brutalizing of wars and revolts, and the ravages of pollution, so more necessary restoration was now under way.

I was in China in 1980 with my two sisters and brother as part of a two-week pilgrimage to our old home. The pilgrimage completed, we parted company in Hong Kong. My older sister, Rosa, had never traveled through Europe, and it was now or never, so we boarded the plane together for Athens.

In Athens, we could see the Parthenon from our hotel room. It was covered with scaffolding. What weather and wars had failed to do in 2,500 years, pollution had accomplished in just a few.

Our next stop was Paris. Jeanette Evans, whom we've known since college days, met us, gave us a swift and amazingly comprehensive tour of Paris, and then took us to her and her husband Bob's home near Versailles. After a night's sleep, we toured Versailles—that is, we walked through a small part of it.

Versailles, which was completed in 1689 after around thirty years of construction, has to be seen to be believed! In the 1700s the Royal Chapel was added, completed in time for the marriage of Louis XVI to Marie Antoinette. And wouldn't you know—the chapel was covered with scaffolding.

We drove the forty miles to Chartres to see its great cathedral, which is one of the finest examples of the French Gothic cathedrals. Once more we found scaffolding.

From Paris we flew to London where even a whirlwind tour

is better than no tour at all—especially if it includes Westminster Abbey. As we approached the exquisite abbey, so alive with history, what did we see? You've already guessed: scaffolding.

Is that the way the world sees the church?

The church is scarred by wars, buffeted by storms, and eroded by pollution, and God is at work restoring His own, repairing, cleaning, purifying. He sees the end from the beginning. He sees us *complete in Christ.* The day will come when *"we shall be like Him."*

But in the meantime, the world sees mainly the scaffolding.

71 · · · · · The Church

"The church is the only society in the world that exists solely for its non-members."

—ARCHBISHOP TEMPLE

· · · · · ⤐⤐ · · · · ·

"What a travesty when the Christian church tries to cultivate inoffensiveness."

—DR. JAMES STUART
of Edinburgh

· · · · · ⤐⤐ · · · · ·

"As for the general view that the church was discredited by the war,—they might as well say that the ark was discredited by the flood. When the world goes wrong, it proves that the church is right."

—G. K. CHESTERTON

· · · · · ⤐⤐ · · · · ·

"You complain bitterly of a dead ministry in your bounds . . . A living ministry is not indispensable to a parish. All our parishes ought to have it and we ought to see to it that they get it, but neither the conversion of sinners, nor the sanctification and comfort of God's saints, is tied up to any man's lips. You will read your unread Bibles more: you will buy more good books: you will meet more in private

converse and prayer: and it will not be bad for you for a season to look
above the pulpit and to look Jesus Christ Himself more immediately in
the face!"

"'In your sore famine of the water of life, run your pipe right up
to the fountain.'"

—RUTHERFORD
to the parishioners of Kilmalcolm

72 · · · · When We See

When we see
faulty, trying "saints,"
(ourselves the guiltiest,
no doubt)
forgive us, Lord,
for our complaints;
and help us never
to forget,
whatever else, Lord,
You're about,
You have not finished
with us
—yet.

73 · · · · Coming Home

"I shall miss Mother this Christmas," the clerk in the Asheville store told me. Her mother had died recently, and this would be the first Christmas without her.

"I used to go home in the evenings, and we'd have such good times together."

The day they put her in the hospital, the doctor told the children they would have to stay out of her room in order for her to rest and get adjusted.

"So I stayed out in the hall," she continued, "waiting . . . listening. Finally I could stand it no longer, and I went in.

"'I thought you'd never come!' Mother said."

Blinking back the tears, the clerk added, with a smile,

"You know, I'm thinking they'll be the first words she'll say to me when I get to Heaven!"

· · · · · ⟶∽⟨⟩ · · · · ·

"Precious in the sight of the Lord is the death of his saints."
—PSALM 116:15

Why?

I've never understood this verse.

Then this past spring, we were getting ready for visits from the children, culminating in a three-day Bell Family Reunion.

There were curtains to be replaced, pictures to hang, meals to plan, some painting to be done.

And all the while, down deep inside there was a happy glow, a growing excitement. It has always been this way since the children left home—whether to boarding school or to marry—the return brought a joy they will understand only when their children grow up, leave, and come home again.

Then I realized I have been looking at death from my perspective, not from God's point of view.

Just as *"there is joy in the presence of the angels of God over one sinner that repenteth,"* so too there is joy in Heaven over each child of God coming home.

This is what my friend, the clerk, was saying.

74 · · · · Expecting Rain

"Looks like rain on the way," Bill announced that day in Florida, eyeing the one suspicious cloud on the horizon. "Let's head north."

And gathering up his dictaphone and a pile of unanswered mail, he herded us all into the car and eased onto A1A heading north.

We had planned our afternoon together on the beach as a family, before joining Lee and Betty Fisher in their home for a dinner of Lee's famous fresh fried fish bits and hush puppies.

Arriving at the Sebastian Inlet, we started to stop. Those of us on the right of the car noted the crowds on the beach. Bill, at the wheel, looked up at the cloud in the sky. It looked closer.

"Let's keep going," Bill said. And we did.

Miles further north we came on a lovely stretch of beach—deserted. So we piled out and settled down while Bill, a few yards off, dictated letters. We were just beginning to soak up the sun when Bill said, "Here comes the cloud. Hurry. Let's get to Lee and Betty's. It's going to rain."

We gathered our blankets and beach bags and discovered why the beach was deserted. It was, and by then we were, covered with tar.

We arrived a bit early at Lee and Betty's.

"Where's my dictaphone and dictation?" Bill asked. A careful search revealed nothing.

"Where do you remember seeing it last?" I asked.

"On top of the car."

So we drove back slowly, everyone searching the roadsides for some sign of a dictaphone and letters. Here and there a page fluttered among the weeds. No dictaphone.

But Lee's fish and hush puppies had never been better.

Incidentally, it never rained.

75 · · · · Prayers Are Answered!

None of the sons would darken a church. They could not have been less interested.

Stephen Harcourt's last days were heavy with longing for his sons.

"Oh Lord," Stephen would pray, *"grant that, when my time comes, my death may be so serene and triumphant, that my boys may see how good a thing it is to be a Christian!"*

When the old man's time came, the sons were all present; but he passed away in utter darkness, his body racked with pain and his mind haunted by the most frightful fears. It looked as if his prayer had been a mockery. But listen!

And F. W. Boreham, who in his book *The Fiery Crag* brought us thus far, now tells us—as Paul Harvey would say—"The Rest of the Story!"

But listen!

"If," said one of his sons to his brothers, *"if father, being the man he was, found death so terrible, how will it be with us?"*

And they all became Christians.

And, concludes Boreham, *"Jeremiah learned that it is not only when our heroes come back in triumph that the Kingdom of God goes forward. Even when our prayers seem all unanswered and our champions are defeated, the great cause is just as surely marching to its radiant goal."*

76 · · · · Spiritual BO

"Self," my friend Elizabeth Strachan said to me with more accuracy than delicacy, "self is spiritual BO."

The more I have thought about that, and the longer I have lived, the more I am convinced she was right.

The people who have affected my life most deeply and influenced it for good have seldom, if ever, been aware of the fact. On the other hand, people who think themselves a blessing seldom are. (There is a difference between being a help and being a blessing.) Self-conscious goodness is a contradiction in terms. Someone has pointed out that it is "I" that changes goodness into goodiness.

"When the Son of man shall come in His glory," Jesus tells us, *"and all the holy angels with Him, then shall He sit upon the throne of His glory: and before Him shall be gathered all nations: and He shall separate them one from another, as a shepherd divideth his sheep from the goats: and He shall set the sheep on His right hand, but the goats on the left."*

Then the King said to the sheep, *"I was ahungered, and you gave me meat: I was thirsty, and you gave me drink: I was a stranger, and you took me in: naked, and you clothed me: I was sick, and you visited me: I was in prison, and you came unto me."*

But then, terrifyingly, He said to the goats, *"Depart from me, you cursed, into everlasting fire, prepared for the devil and his angels."* He continued, saying the very opposite of what He had said to the sheep. These goats had ignored His every need—which, He explained, were the needs of the least of His brethren.

The point is, those who had ministered to His needs were as unaware of their goodness and kindness as those who were indifferent were unaware of their indifference.

136

Perhaps this is why Jesus warned us against doing alms before men. And not letting our right hand know what the left is doing.

T. Dixon, Jr., writing of Abraham Lincoln described him as *"a man who was always doing merciful things stealthily as other men do crimes."*

· · · · · ⤳ · · · · ·

A friend remarked of a stingy relative, "He doesn't want his right hand to know that his left hand is doing nothing."

77·····God, Bless All Young Mothers

God,
bless all young mothers
at end of day.
Kneeling wearily with each
small one
to hear them pray.
Too tired to rise when done . . .
and yet they do;
longing just to sleep
one whole night through.
Too tired to sleep . . .
Too tired to pray . . .
God,
bless all young mothers
at close of day.

78 · · · · The Mender

He had built for himself a great house on one of the Caribbean islands. It is a thing to behold. Tall rusty iron columns, collected and resurrected with an ingenious homemade device. This Great House is a masterpiece of salvaged materials.

A collector and seller of scrap metal as well as antiques, he was also fascinated with broken bits and pieces of china dug from his front yard. His friends, John and June Cash, laughingly remarked it was the first time they had heard of a yard sale where the man had sold the yard itself. Carefully he fitted and glued the pieces together. Few ever came out whole. They remained simply the collection of one who cared.

When I expressed interest, he gave me a blue-and-white plate, carefully glued together—pieces missing.

"You remind me of God," I said. By the look on his face, I knew I had shocked him, and I hurriedly explained.

"God pieces back broken lives lovingly. Sometimes a piece is irretrievably lost. But still He gathers what He can and restores us.

"Perhaps it gives pleasure to no one else, but to Him."

· · · · · ⚬⚬⚬ · · · · ·

It stands on the bookshelf at the side of the hall by our bedroom door. A constant reminder that God cares about broken lives, broken people. Lovingly, painstakingly, He puts them back together. *"He restores my soul."*

Mary Magdalene . . .

The woman taken in adultery . . .

"Go . . . tell My disciples and Peter . . ."

Some may be of no practical, human use because of some missing piece, but they can be a comforting reminder that God cares deeply about broken people and wants to piece them back together—painstakingly and with love.

And God, the Mender of broken lives, will take pleasure in them.

"No faith can have vitality or hope that does not hold that we are somehow the better for our failures and our falls, however much they may have devastated our life and influence, with whatever shame and reproach they may have wasted our days."

—BENSON'S *Life of Ruskin*

79 · · · · Carried

The strapping young father hoisted his son to his shoulders where he sat happily, each leg firmly held in one of his father's strong hands. From this vantage point, the little guy had a breadth of view he could not otherwise have enjoyed.

He was also safe—safe from the blistering hot sand, the onrushing waves, even from occasional sharp shells or broken glass. And he could go indefinitely without getting tired. His short legs wouldn't have to run to keep up with his dad's. On those broad shoulders "keeping up" was no problem.

I was watching the pair from our friends' lovely condominium, and I thought of the aging Moses, who reminded the children of Israel in Deuteronomy 1:31: *"The Lord thy God bare thee, as a man doth bear his son."* God also assures us in Isaiah 46:4: *"And even to your old age I am he; and even to hoar hairs will I carry you: I have made, and I will bear; even I will carry, and will deliver you."*

Being lifted up and carried so securely is not limited to a little boy on a beach; it also includes those of old age with gray hair.

That strong young father on the beach was a reassuring reminder that there is One who lifts and carries us. That One is our heavenly Father Himself.

80 · · · · The Unrelieved Complaining

The unrelieved complaining
of the wind across the ridge,
rising of a sudden,
to a wild and lonesome roar,
like the sad, sustained resounding
of the surf upon some shore;
leaves my own heart strangely pounding:
—as if I'd heard God sighing
for a world astray and dying,
and somewhere, a lost soul crying,
wanting more.

81 · · · · · Horn Blowers

I started to get in my car and found I had locked it and left the keys in the ignition.

I was doing a little shopping in Escondido, California, before heading back to Pauma Valley.

So I went into the men's clothing department and found a wire clothes hanger. Putting my purse on the roof of the car, I bent the clothes hanger double, leaving the curved hook at the end.

Easing it through the crack in the window, I inched it slowly down . . . down.

Carefully I succeeded in easing the hook under the door lock.

Just as I was about to pull up, I felt eyes on me. You don't have to see eyes to feel them.

I turned. Parked just behind me was a car full of people watching me.

"They think I'm breaking in," I said to myself. Quickly, carefully, I gave the coat hanger a jerk. Up came the lock. I opened the door and took off with as much quiet dignity as I could muster.

They honked at me.

Ignoring them, I circled the lot. Looking carefully left, I turned right on the street.

A car, passing me, honked.

People are really acting strange, I thought, for what was usually an exceptionally friendly town.

I drew up at the red light.

A car pulled up alongside, its occupants waving. I smiled.

But they were pointing.

"Your pocketbook," they shouted. "It's on top of the car."

82 · · · · Self-Indulgent and Addicted

Lunch had just begun when our guest casually announced his family had the day before sold a well-known product, clearing $13 million. Before we even had time to choke on the soup, he exclaimed, "Guess what I discovered in the Bible today!" And he proceeded to treat us to a spiritual feast. It was that way whenever we were with him. He delighted in the Lord and His Word.

The Septuagint translation of Psalm 37:4 reads, "*Indulge thyself with delight in the Lord.*" It is a joy to meet Christians who indulge themselves with delight in the Lord until they are full to overflowing with spiritual refreshment!

There are also the addicted. Paul refers in I Corinthians 16:15 to certain believers who had "*addicted themselves to the ministry of the saints.*"

We knew such a family of Christians in Wheaton when we were there attending college. A large and generous family, the Lanes lived in a large and generous Victorian mansion. Every Sunday they laid out a full-course, sit-down dinner for forty to sixty people—mostly the children of missionaries, but also some who just happened to need a good meal.

Another friend, who lived under a hostile atheistic regime, knit for others. She could turn out a sweater a week—even "long johns." With bitter winters and no central heating, these provided excellent thermal underwear.

One old Irish friend, Mrs. Moore, from China lived in a little room in a retirement home in Belfast. I stopped to see her on a visit to Northern Ireland, and there, in the center of the room, was her work desk: a folding table. "Let me show you what I'm doing," she said enthusiastically, the blue eyes I knew as a child still lovely, still twinkling.

144

On the table was an odd assortment of empty plastic bottles, boxes, and bits and pieces no one else wanted. "I send these to my missionary friends to pass around. It helps in a clinic when a wee child has to have a shot." To those who have nothing, even an empty plastic bottle is a treasure.

Each of these individuals was *"addicted . . . to the ministry of the saints."*

"Indulging themselves with delight in the Lord" and "addicted to the ministry of the saints"—what a combination!

83 · · · · Journal

Monday, September 14, 1970

For several days I've been bone tired, and heavy spirited, easily irritable, negative—just not good company—for God, me, or anybody. Time of year? End of a busy summer? Spiritual recession? I don't know.

But I excused myself early from the kids and their friends last night and went to bed when Ned did.

At 4:30 I awoke and got up briefly but was still so utterly tired I lay back down—praying. In half an hour I felt better, so got up and made a cup of coffee.

And as I sat with Him—reading mainly from the Psalms, just thinking of Him, His love, His forgiveness, His understanding— all the tiredness and heaviness went away. By 7:00 I was refreshed and ready for the day!

84····Leave a Little Light On

Leave a little light on
somewhere, in some room,
dark rainy days;
where, in the deepening gloom,
I, damped and greyed
by weather, might
in some unexpected place
glimpse warmth and cheer.
Those who feel that light
is utilitarian only,
have never known
the desolation dusk can bring
to being lonely.

85 · · · · "They've Got More Money"

I was brought up to understand that there are three questions one never asks: How old? How much? What kind of operation?

That July 29 I got up at 4:45 A.M. along with some seven or eight hundred million other people to watch the Royal Wedding. It was an unforgettable six hours of pomp and circumstance. The pageantry, the responsive crowds, the young bride's loveliness, the groom's character and relaxed demeanor, were all threaded together with the sometimes bumbling explanations by American commentators aided or corrected by their British counterparts.

To me, the grandest moment came when, at the request of Prince Charles, the great congregation and choir in St. Paul's Cathedral sang "Christ Is Made the Sure Foundation." It would have been worth whatever the wedding cost just to have eight hundred million people hear that great hymn!

What followed was a variety of interviews that filled the time while the bride and groom, with their families and friends, had a meal in Buckingham Palace before leaving for Broadlands and the beginning of their honeymoon.

"Is it true," the interviewer asked Mrs. Reagan, "that the Steuben glass urn cost $75,000?"

"And have you chipped in to pay for the gate?" a young girl was asked in the tiny village of Tetbury, where the country residence of the Prince and Princess of Wales stands. The surrounding villages had gone together to have a new wrought iron gate made to replace the old one, which was broken down.

"Yes I 'ave," the girl replied with a smile.

"Not yet. But will do," the next responded.

"No," growled one man. "They've got more money than I've got. Why should I?"

148

George Macdonald wrote, "*But it is not the rich man only who is under the dominion of things; they too are slaves who, having no money, are unhappy from lack of it.*"

We have put a price tag on everything but the human soul and its relationship to God who made it. And a wise man once said, "*He who has God and has everything, has no more than he who has God and has nothing.*"

86 · · · · Contentment

"He appears to have been a sunny, playful man," wrote C. S. Lewis of George Macdonald, "deeply appreciative of all really beautiful and delicious things that money can buy, and no less deeply content to do without them."

—George Macdonald, An Anthology
BY C. S. LEWIS

· · · · · ⤸⤹ · · · · ·

Later in the Anthology, George Macdonald himself says:

"Let me, if I may, be ever welcomed to my room in winter by a glowing hearth, in summer by a vase of flowers; if I may not, let me think how nice they would be, and bury myself in my work. I do not think that the road to contentment lies in despising what we have not got. Let us acknowledge all good, all delight that the world holds, and be content without it."

—George Macdonald, An Anthology
BY C. S. LEWIS

87. · · · Thoughts on Prayer

Men of God, whose prayers are recorded for us in the Bible, never read a book on prayer, never went to a seminar on prayer, never heard a sermon on prayer. They just prayed.

Satan fears prayer because God hears prayer. Satan will stop at nothing to distract a person from praying or to get him to postpone praying or, failing that, to discourage him in his praying.

The center of power, it has been said, is to be found not in the summit meetings, the peace conferences, or the United Nations, but where a child of God prays for God's will to be done in his life, in his home, and in the world about him.

We cannot pray and remain the same. We cannot pray and have our homes remain the same. We cannot pray and have the world about us remain the same. God has decreed to act in response to prayer. "Ask," He commands us. And Satan trembles for fear we will.

Alexander the Great once gave a poor man a city, and when he modestly refused it as too great for him, Alexander replied, *"The business is not what thou art fit to receive but what it becometh me to give."*

William Barclay has said that *"in praying for those we love we must remember: (1) the love of God that wants the best for them; (2) the wisdom of God that knows what is best for them; and (3) the power of God that can accomplish it."*

"Heaven must be full of answers to prayers for which no one ever bothered to ask."

—CAMERON THOMPSON

Start where you are, as you are, about whatever concerns you, whatever is lying most heavily on your heart, whatever is irritating or frustrating you at present.

Suggestion: Keep a prayer list (small dime-store notebook or an inexpensive diary would do just fine). Make your requests specific and date them. Then date the answer. Like the ungrateful lepers of Luke 17:17, we tend to forget.

It may be impossible to date the answers to certain requests. For instance, if I pray for patience, I will not find that on such and such a date I suddenly became patient. But if I pray for guidance in a particular problem, or the conversion of a friend, or the resolving of some apparently hopeless difficulty, recording the answer as well as the request will be a cause for worship and a means of strengthening my faith.

Be pointed. Be persistent. Be patient. But pray.

Do you remember things you prayed about as a child? Like for a lizard, or a puppy, or a bat (I did—the kind that fly. A very special one to me, I shared with an older missionary who laughed. I could understand the laughter, but I never shared it again.)

There was the time our hospital business manager's two children were kidnapped by bandits and held for ransom. The father did not have the money, and it was against Mission policy to pay ransoms.

But everyone—missionaries, Chinese friends, and coworkers, even we children—prayed.

In a few weeks they were back—without ransom—a thing unheard of in China then. (Two years ago I got a snapshot from the older of the children—now a rugged man in his sixties.)

We had a man who helped us at one point when I was a child. He had gone A.W.O.L. from the Chinese Army which promptly went after him, found him, and cut off his ears (the customary punishment for going A.W.O.L.).

So, Ma Er wore his hair in bangs in front and down over where his ears had been—like a girl. He was a terrible tease, with a sunny, kind disposition. We children loved him dearly.

He was not a Christian. I finally left to go to North Korea, to boarding school, Ma Er's name still on my prayer list.

Years later I learned that he had given his heart to the Lord and became a sincere believer.

Be pointed. Be persistent. Be patient. But pray.

> *"In weakness and in want we call*
> *On Thee for whom the heavens are small."*
> —J. G. WHITTIER
> "All Things Are Thine"

88 · · · · The Possibilities in Family Prayer

When do you have family prayers? Have you ever considered that a good time might be after the evening television network news? Or after the morning news? Not only could we pray for our families and friends and local problems then, but we could bring to the Lord the various crises and events we have just seen portrayed on the screen.

What a difference it might make if each day, as newscasts conclude, a great wave of prayer could ascend to God from across the country on behalf of those in trouble and those making trouble!

We could pray by name not only for the individuals involved, but for each newscaster, each commentator.

Sidlow Baxter once said, *"Men may spurn our appeal, reject our message, oppose our arguments, despise our persons, but they are helpless against our prayers.*

"The greater the diameter of our knowledge of human need, the larger will be the circumference of our petitions."

John Newton, who wrote the well-loved hymn "Amazing Grace," also wrote:

> *"Come, my soul, thy suit prepare,*
> *Jesus loves to answer prayer:*
> *He Himself has bid thee pray,*
> *Therefore will not say thee nay.*
>
> *Thou art coming to a King,*
> *Large petitions with thee bring;*
> *For His grace and power are such*
> *None can ever ask too much."*

89····Missing the Children

"Only Pudge has joined a religious group in India," read the letter, "gone for three-and-a-half years. Do you know anyone there who could reach her? We haven't heard in eight months. Except for the deep pain of her loss, my life is wonderful now . . . It's been an unbelievable experience but the pain is pushed down."

The letter was from a dear friend who has suffered incredibly. Yet I'm sure it is the loss of this one daughter that has caused the deepest hurt.

Soon after reading that, I watched a young author being interviewed on TV about a book she has written on missing children. I was shocked to learn that children seven years old and above are considered accountable by the law. The thirteen- to fourteen-year-olds are most certainly accountable. If they are missing, it is generally assumed they have run away. Not only is there often little help from the police, nor any central clearinghouse for tracking the lost, but the parents themselves are frequently suspect; did they do away with the children?

In any case, concern and hurt over missing children are all too often combined with feelings of guilt. One can more easily handle death and gradually learn to accept it, but not this.

And then I recalled 1954. We were in London for three months' mission in the old Harringay Arena in dreary north London.

A friend had offered to give me a round-trip ticket back to the U.S. so that in the middle of that period I could return home to break the long separation from the children. When the first month of the mission was completed, however, Bill felt he needed me and urged me to stay.

Watching God work in lives was a tremendous privilege, but

underneath was a growing longing to see the children. I couldn't bear to look at their pictures on the dresser, and when bedtime came with little more than a quick, "Dear God, please bless each one," I would dive into bed and try to fall asleep.

My letters home must have betrayed how I felt, because in one of her letters Mother told of Anne praying: "Dear God, please bless Mommy and help her not to be so homesick for us." They were quite happy and content. It was I who was miserable.

But it taught me a lesson I have never forgotten. I thought about it when I read the letter from my young friend. I thought about it when I watched the interview on television. When we are away from God, He misses us far more than we miss Him.

90····He Sang Atop the Old Split Rail

He sang atop the old split rail
all while it thundered,
raindrops pelting him like hail;
and I wondered:
how one small, vulnerable bird,
defying deafening thunder,
could make itself sweetly heard
—and still I wonder—

91·····Thirsting

"*Isaac was the son of a great father,*" F. W. Boreham wrote, "*and the father of a great son.*" And Isaac was more; he was a digger of wells.

One has to live in the desert to fully appreciate wells—especially when one's flocks and herds depend on the water they provide. "*Deep wells tap the life-giving water beneath the surface of the earth, but the animals cannot reach it. The shepherd must draw the water with a bucket and offer each animal a drink*" (GILBERT BEERS, Book of Life).

In John 4, Jesus, wearied by walking in the heat of the noonday sun, sat beside a well that Isaac's son Jacob had dug centuries before. It was in Samaria, and a woman came at midday to get water. He knew women in that time and place did their water carrying in the cool of the mornings and evenings. This one chose the heat of noon for a reason; she was a moral outcast. Jesus saw right through her pretense. He always does.

He asked her for a drink. Imagine—the Great Shepherd asking a little black sheep for a drink! But it worked. Why, she wondered suspiciously, did He, a Jew, ask a favor of a Samaritan? (You can read the background of those Jewish-Samaritan tensions in II Kings 17:24–41.)

"If you knew the gift of God and Who it is who asks you for a drink, you would have asked Him and He would have given you living water."

Deftly she changed the subject. "Sir," she said, "You have nothing to draw with and the water is deep. Where can You get this living water?"

We have now shifted gears completely. From H_2O we have gone to the Water of Life. Here was a thirsty Shepherd, an even thirstier sheep, and many more in that village coming to drink of Him.

Since that day there have been many thirsty sheep—and perhaps shepherds, too—who thought they could improve on that Water. William Cowper wrote:

"Letting down buckets into empty wells and growing old with the drawing nothing up."

92 ···· When No Voice Can Be Heard

The cat had kittens on the trundle bed in the downstairs guest room.

We didn't think that was such a good idea, so we collected them and placed them on rags in a cardboard box in front of the kitchen fireplace until we could come up with something more suitable.

But the mother cat had a mind of her own. We watched with amusement as she entered the kitchen silently, stood on her back legs, front legs on the box, sniffing for her babies. Then leaping nimbly over the side, she checked them over, picked one up by the back of the neck, leaped out, and quietly returned it to the trundle bed.

This was repeated till all that was left was the runt of the litter.

She did not come back. She may have been exhausted from her efforts, or she may have been busy playing lunch counter to the others.

We waited.

Finally the tiny scrap in the bottom of the box let out more of a squeak than a mew. It was almost a nonsound.

Instantly, soundlessly, the mother cat appeared, bounded in and out of the box, the littlest kitten in her mouth, and carried it back to the guest room.

Three doors, two rooms, and two hallways away, and yet she heard.

· · · · · ∽❦⌒ · · · · ·

The Great Dane had her first litter of pups (two, to be exact) under the lilac bush outside the kitchen window.

After second thoughts she picked up the larger one and carried it to the dog house (around two sides of the house), but being irresponsible, she forgot to return for the second.

After awhile number two pup got hungry. It made the sort of noise newborn pups make, and a very weak one at that.

I could hear the mother coming before I saw her. Galloping like a clap of thunder, she skidded to a stop, and gently lifting the little left-behind by the back of its what-was-supposed-to-be neck, she carried it to join the other.

. . . . . ∽⤳◯ . . . . .

In neither case was it even a full-fledged cry . . .

Nor are our prayers necessarily full-fledged prayers—or even articulated cries for help.

According to the Bible, God responds to our sighs, our tears, our murmurs—even our longings can be interpreted as prayer.

John Trapp said in commenting on Psalm 145, *"The Lord is near to all that call upon him; yea, he can feel breath when no voice can be heard for faintness."*

93 ···· Wondering About Paul

My sister, Rosa, and I were sitting in a little sidewalk cafe north of Athens.

In Sounion, which perches on the top of the cape southeast of Athens, are the ruins of the once lovely temple dedicated to the sea god Poseidon, and we wanted to see them. The apostle Paul must have sailed past this cape on his second missionary journey and looked up to see the tall white columns gracing the top.

Sidewalk cafes are friendlier and more informal than tourist hotels, and this one was no exception. Sitting at a neighboring table was a genial English couple, who struck up a conversation about all they had seen. "You know," they commented, "one wonders, after traveling around this place, if a man named Paul didn't live here after all."

The mind goes back in time two thousand years to an ancient Athens that was smaller and more beautiful than the Athens of today. It was *"a provincial university city, the home of art treasures"* (OTTO F. A. MEINARDUS, *Paul in Greece*).

It was dominated by the Acropolis with its magnificent temples, the largest and most magnificent being the famous Parthenon. These buildings had already been standing for several hundred years when Paul arrived.

An ancient proverb declared that there were more gods in Athens than men, and wherever the apostle looked, there were gods—in temples, in niches, on pedestals, on street corners. Paul even discovered a temple to the unknown god.

Paul saw that the city was wholly given over to idolatry, and his spirit was *"exasperated"* (NEB). He disputed with the religious leaders, with devout persons, with those he met in the marketplace. Then he took on certain philosophers of the Epicureans and the Stoics.

In the days of Paul, the Council of the Areopagus had authority over all matters pertaining to the religious life of the city, and it was because of this that Paul was invited to appear before them. Here he delivered his famous speech that changed the course of history, though the change was not sudden but gradual. When he spoke of the resurrection of the dead, some mocked; others said they wanted to hear him again on the matter.

But when Paul left Athens, he left behind at least two believers: a woman named Damaris, about whom we know nothing, and Dionysius the Areopagite.

Then silence fell. We know only that a small Christian community did develop, and it grew in spite of the paganism that continued to flourish around it. By A.D. 408–50, several temples in Athens had been converted into churches. During the reign of Justinian (A.D. 527–65), the Parthenon itself was turned into a church, and remained one for two hundred years. At about the same time, the Erechtheum atop the Acropolis was also converted into a church.

There are churches in Athens today dedicated to the apostle Paul, though it is not Paul but his first Athenian convert, Dionysius the Areopagite, who is venerated as the patron saint of Athens.

Today, two thousand years later, the temples are in various stages of ruin. And who can name the gods to whom they were erected? Who can name the members of the Areopagus? Who, aside from scholars, knows the form of government in Greece at that time?

Yet, "after traveling around this place, one wonders if a man named Paul didn't live here after all."

94 ···· Satan Speaks

Satan speaks:
Herein
lies my cleverest ploy,
Hell's greatest power,
this plot
that fills me with Satanic joy:
convincing those within our
jurisdiction, that somehow
I am not.

95···· Great Expectations

Anne called. "I'm mailing you a booklet," she said excitedly. "It's all about why Jesus will return for believers September 11, 12, or 13.

"Now don't laugh!" she urged. "Just read it. And hurry or you might not have time to finish it," she teased.

The booklet arrived at a period when life was full speed ahead.

But I made myself sit down and read until the writer's scholarship lost me. He sounded like he knew quite a bit about the Jewish feasts, Daniel's seventy weeks, and all the rest. Only Jesus had specifically warned against such predictions, as Anne agreed. It was with mixed feelings that I anticipated Christ's possible imminent return.

I had an awful lot to do, left undone, including this book.

I sure would hate for anyone to find how disorganized this Pack Rat is.

Yet the mere anticipation of heading Home filled life with an expectant glow.

But before long I put it down and went back to this month's priority—*Legacy of a Pack Rat*.

Our local paper picked up on the story of the prediction. Anne told me of some churches being crowded (good!). Some people were beginning to realize Jesus is *real* and one day will return, as He said, and were committing their hearts and lives to Him (good!). Others were selling their property (what would they do with the money, we wondered?).

The day passed, uneventfully.

I called Anne.

"You still there?" I asked.

"I'm still here," she laughed.

"I was afraid you might have been raptured, and I'd been left behind."

But we both agreed that with the world in the mess it's in, it can't be too far off.

Then I recalled a certain poem. After a brief search, I found it in William Barclay's *Commentary on Matthew.**

A black poet wrote:

> "There's a king and a captain high,
> And He's coming by and by,
> And He'll find me hoeing cotton when He comes.
> You can hear His legions charging in the regions
>   of the sky,
> And He'll find me hoeing cotton when He comes.
> There's a Man they thrust aside,
> Who was tortured till He died,
> And He'll find me hoeing cotton when He comes.
> He was hated and rejected,
> He was scorned and crucified,
> And He'll find me hoeing cotton when He comes.
> When He comes! When He comes!
> He'll be crowned by saints and angels when He comes.
> They'll be shouting out Hosanna! to the Man that
>   men denied,
> And I'll kneel among my cotton when He comes."

*William Barclay, *The Gospel of Matthew*, vol. 2 (Philadelphia: The Westminster Press, 1957; Edinburgh, Scotland: The Saint Andrew Press, 1957), p. 351.

96····I Am a Primitive

I am a primitive.
   I love
primordial silences
   that reign
unbroken over ridge
   and plain,
unspoiled by civilization's roar.
I love the lonesome sound
   of wind,
the final crashing
   of a tree,
the wash of waves
   upon the shore,
wind . . . thunder—and
   the pouring rain
are symphonies to me.

97 · · · · God Is Ingenious

I lifted the phone receiver to place a call, and to my surprise, music from our local Christian radio station floated out of it. Bewildered, I replaced the receiver and tried again. More music.

So much for the phone call.

A few days later I was chatting with a clerk in a jewelry store in a nearby town.

"Here's one you'll never believe," she said, leaning across the display case. I leaned forward to listen.

A regular customer from a neighboring town had not dropped by for sometime. When she finally came in, she was on crutches.

"What on earth . . . ?" the clerk wanted to know.

And the friend told her. They were having some landscaping done in the yard with a bulldozer. She had slipped somehow and had broken her leg. While recuperating, she found herself alone in the house one Sunday, propped up in bed. Lonely and bored, she decided to call a friend and found the phone was just out of reach. She made several swipes at it but only succeeded in knocking it off the cradle, onto the floor, out of reach. And from the receiver came "The Hour of Decision."

She wasn't interested in listening to "The Hour of Decision," but she couldn't reach the phone, so she had no choice. She was a captive audience.

"And would you know!" the clerk said to me. "She came in here to tell me she had asked the Lord Jesus into her life and heart and to make her a new person. And I, who've known her a long time, could tell that He had!"

If I hadn't experienced the first, I would have questioned the latter.

To say that God is ingenious is an understatement!

98 · · · · If I Lived Within the Sound

If I lived within the sound
of the sea's relentless yearning,
my soul would rise and fly to seek
what the sea longs for—unable to speak;
aware, as I go, of Him everywhere:
in my heart, in the clouds, the cold wet air.
And my soul would worship in joyful prayer,
receding as the waves recede,
returning with the waves returning,
reaching up—as for Him feeling—
then with the waves kneeling . . .
                    kneeling . . .
                        kneeling . . .

99···Love Covers

My pet rabbit died rather abruptly (as pet rabbits have a way of doing). It was a forlorn eight-year-old who lovingly buried him beside the sandpile in our yard in China. Then every day I dug him up to see how he was getting along. The last time I saw him he was green.

The principle of "love covers" versus "investigative reporting" in Christian magazines is being kicked about like a ball on a soccer field. The opposing teams are the Pros versus the Cons. At the moment the Pros are ahead.

Thinking about our greater mission family in China while I was growing up, I remembered gratefully one occasion when someone fell—and how quickly, quietly, and effectively that fall was dealt with. Then love covered. It was not, like my pet rabbit, dug up again. I thought about our own family through the years and how, on occasion, situations had to be faced and dealt with. And buried.

I think of churches that wisely and compassionately deal the same way and of Paul's plea for a censured Christian he felt had had enough: *"So that contrariwise ye ought rather to forgive him and comfort him, lest perhaps such a one should be swallowed up with overmuch sorrow"* (II CORINTHIANS 2:7).

There is a school where a student who needs to be disciplined has to do a certain number of laps around the athletic field; how many depends on the seriousness of the offense. But if another student taunts him or so much as refers to it later, he receives the same punishment—doubled.

There will always be those rare occasions when some heresy, some cult, or some con game operating under the name of Christianity needs to be exposed so as to warn others. But that is something different. It seldom involves the trip-ups and tragedies of true believers. In "the family," flagrant sins should be dealt with promptly, compassionately, privately. Then silence.

Every cat knows some things need to be buried.

100···He Took His Cross

He took His cross
as best he could
(cross-bearing was
so new to him).
How could he tell
the torturous load
of rough hewn wood
on that rutted road
where he was led,
would saw his shoulder
till it bled;
and then . . .
he fell.

Of all the curious,
crowding round,
who
stepping out, stooped down
to do
what Simon did
long years ago?
—but He, who
staggering beneath our cross,
fell, too.

101 ···· Of Death and Easter

The old pole cabin was past due for a cleaning. The porch and a few rotting logs had been replaced. Now, with the help of the grandchildren, we were about to tackle the inside.

The Monday after Easter had dawned cool and clear. Somehow restoring and repairing seemed to fit in with Easter.

For years we had used the cabin for storage: piles of old car and motorcycle tires, boxes of books, empty cartons, an old Victorian sofa, a crude wooden cradle, a case of dishes, assorted chairs in need of repair, an incredible accumulation of junk—and nests of flying squirrels.

Most of these enchanting and destructive little creatures scrambled for safety as soon as the cleanup began. Then as we started stacking old tires, something exploded from one of them. When we recovered, we found it was a mother flying squirrel, and there in the tire we discovered her colorful, smelly nest (made of colored gift wrapping yarns from our attic, no less!) and two tiny babies.

While we were lifting out one, the other got away, and before we could retrieve him, Toke (the Alaskan malamute) had him for a mid-morning snack.

Later in the day, the grandchildren discovered the carcass of the old wild turkey down in the woods. In great distress, they came to report it, thinking it was a recent kill. I explained that Toke had done that last year. (We knew he was the guilty party as he threw up turkey for two days.)

Toke, never a favorite with the grandchildren, was liked less by the minute.

That afternoon, the grandchildren went exploring. Soon we heard screaming from the girls and shouts of anger from Jonathan.

174

Into the house they boiled—furious but not incoherent. Toke had flushed a mother quail from her nest and eaten three eggs at one gulp.

Easter. New life: trees budding, bloodroot and wild violets carpeting the woods, nests with little new things—like quail eggs and baby flying squirrels. And stalking death in the form of a dog who is part wolf.

Easter—in one small mountain cove—illustrating Easter around the world. Life in the midst of death.

Death, the hideous result of man's rebellion against God. And persisting life—reminders that God sent His Son to die for us and rise again from the dead, that we might have true life in Him. The last enemy that will be destroyed by God is death.

But till He comes again in glory, every Easter season will be marred by the specter of dying.

102 ··· The Caring Heart

"... The supreme characteristic of courtesy is that thoughtfulness for others which is the very heart of Christianity. Schools of etiquette produce it by training; love does it by instinct."
—HENRY DURBANVILLE

· · · · · ∽⌒∾ · · · · ·

A well-known leader of the community was found dead drunk—and in public.

Mr. Allan Emery tells, in his choice book *Turtle On A Fencepost*, how his father sent the chauffeured limousine to pick him up and bring him to the house (the house being a replica of Mount Vernon in Boston).

Allan noticed with concern that his mother had prepared the big guest room. There were fresh flowers on the dresser. And, to Allan's horror, he saw that his mother had made up the handsome four-poster with real linen hemstitched sheets and monogrammed linen pillowcases.

Allan protested to his mother that she knew nothing about drunks—that they got sick and the man would throw up all over the bed, sheets, and antique bedspread.

Looking at her perturbed son, his mother said seriously,

"When he wakes up, he'll feel sick, lonely and ashamed. It is important for him to see immediately that he is our honored guest and that we gave him our best."

She knew he would need all the encouragement he could get.

176

103···Compassion

One of the loveliest words in the Bible is *compassion*. It has been replaced today with *empathy*—if it can be replaced.

The Revised Standard Version uses the words *"to bear gently with."*

Perhaps it is one of those words that the old Puritan scholar John Trapp says, *"cannot be Englished."*

Thomas Goodwin, another great Puritan scholar and one-time Chaplain to Oliver Cromwell, says,

"This great Greek word is extremely emphatical. It means much more than the English rendering 'Who can have compassion' means. For when this great Greek word of the Apostle is rightly rendered, and is rightly laid to heart, it reveals to us that Jesus Christ, our Great High Priest, not only has a great compassion in His heart, but that He has a special and a particular compassion measured out according to every individual man's measure of need, according to every individual man's specialty, and particularity and singularity, and secrecy of need."

104···Good Bait

Each vacation in Caneel Bay, Grady patiently fished off the point below the house. Hour after hour. Using little silver lures. Then they hired a boat and tried stone crabs. They got up early and fished. They went out after dark and fished. In all this time they have only caught three fish—and they were by accident.

We knew the waters were teeming with fish. We could see whole schools of little fish break water and skim like a wave of silver spray across the surface, and we knew a big fish was after them. And we would see the waters churn as a large fish struggled to escape even larger fish.

I took up snorkeling.

Then I understood.

There are thousands of little fish down there. Yellow fish, blue fish, striped fish, spotted fish, purple fish, long, slim needlefish . . . little silvery minnows by the billion. When swimming with the sun behind you, it was like swimming through shimmering liquid silver.

Why then would fish be attracted by artificial bait? You have to offer them something better than what they've got.

105 ··· Offering Christ

Pashi was a student in our local college.

Twenty years ago, and even before, Oriental religion and Hindu mysticism held an irresistible attraction for young would-be intellectuals.

Presented with the claims of Christ, Pashi replied devastatingly, "I would like to believe in Christ. We of India would like to believe in Christ. But we have never seen a Christian who was like Christ."

Come to think of it, neither have I.

We believers are all merely pilgrims in progress, encumbered with disagreeable genes, trying—and in the process being found "trying indeed." There are degrees of saintliness, but the very term *Christ-like* is confusing. Like Him in what way? His ability to heal? To cast out demons? To raise the dead? To cast the money changers out of the Temple? To teach? To face His accusers calmly, silently?

I think basically what is meant by the term *Christ-like* has got to do with His attitude toward His Father's will.

"Lo, I came to do Thy will . . . I delight to do Thy will."

Whatever the true meaning, I was feeling we had somehow let the Lord down rather badly.

So I decided to call our friend and longtime coworker, Dr. Akbar Haqq, a brilliant Christian who used to be President of the Henry Martyn School of Islamic Studies in New Delihi.

"Akbar," I asked when I got him on the phone and explained the problem, "what would you say? How would you answer Pashi?"

"That is quite simple," Akbar said decisively (that's one thing I like about Akbar, he can be so clear, so decisive), "I would tell him,

"'I am not offering you Christians. I am offering you Christ.'"

106···Fear

The shot through the rattlesnake's head had all but demolished it. The rattler was still twisting on the driveway as the family gathered around to see the latest snake kill. Yuro, one of the dogs, eased forward to finish it off, and the snake struck again. The dog jumped back.

Then one of the grandchildren reached out to touch it. Bill grabbed him and held him back, explaining how deadly even a dead snake can be. The young grandson, totally without fear, was determined to grab its tail. Again the mangled head struck out. The boy jumped back, getting the message. Rattlesnakes and copperheads, the only two poisonous snakes in our region, are to be feared.

"Education," wrote Angelo Patri, *"consists in being afraid of the right things."* And snakes are one of them.

We taught our children to be careful with matches and to be respectful of open fire; fear of house fires and forest fires prompts sensible precautions. We also taught the children never to run into the street without first carefully looking both ways; a proper fear of cars is also legitimate—as are accepting rides from strangers, using unprescribed drugs, not wearing helmets when riding motorcycles, breaking the law, and dishonoring one's parents or one's country.

There is one grand, noble fear we are taught from Genesis to Revelation. It is *"fear of the Lord."* This is more than "being scared" (though there is a bit of that in it, too). It is "a reverential trust," not only a fear of offending, but a loving to the point one would not want to offend.

"In the fear of the Lord is strong confidence: and his children shall have a place of refuge."

—Proverbs 14:26

"The fear of the Lord is the beginning of wisdom."
—PSALM 111:10

"O that there were such a heart in them, that they would fear me, and keep all my commandments always, that it might be well with them, and with their children for ever!"
—DEUTERONOMY 5:29

"To guard against all such blasphemous chumminess with the Almighty, the Bible talks of the fear of the Lord—not to scare us but to bring us to awesome attention before the overwhelming grandeur of God."
—EUGENE H. PETERSON
A Long Obedience in the Same Direction

We live in a world wracked by fears and anxieties. The following appeared in *Le Monde* (Paris) in the summer of 1981:

"A Long Bastille Day Weekend
"In France, overheated and overcrowded prisons are about to explode. In Northern Ireland, IRA inmates are dying one after the other. In El Salvador, it's murder unlimited. In Chile, 'order' reigns. In Asia, the refugees keep looking for refuge. Poland fears the summer. Afghanistan resists in silence, Iran rants on. Purges are under way just about everywhere.
"The South is hungry, the North is afraid.
"Happy weekend, everybody!"

But God reassures His church in Revelation, *"Fear none of those things which are to happen."* We are to fear only the Lord.

It is the fear of God that puts all other fears in proper perspective.

107···Spooked!

They were getting spooked, George and Corenne, our friends and helpers. We were on a trip, and they found the TV in our bedroom blaring.

So George, canny about things electrical, removed the remote control to the kitchen.

But the next day again he found it on.

A few days later, Corenne, getting ready for our return, was startled to hear the TV suddenly turn on loud and clear.

"Did it ever happen when you were here?" they asked. I, as confused as they, said it had never happened when I was there.

····· ∽ɔ⌒ ·····

Then it did.

I was in our bedroom. The phone rang. Instantaneously our TV set came on. Since I'm not electrically or mechanically minded, such things are beyond me.

But I could wish that I, as a Christian, could be so spiritually attuned to God that when someone is hurting or in need, He could, as it were, by remote control (an impulse, a suggestion from a friend, a Bible verse recalled, a divine "nudge") "turn me on."

P.S. I was watching the news one night when the channels began to switch. I was puzzled till I realized one of the German shepherd dogs with me was scratching himself. Each time he scratched, the channel changed. I am still puzzled.

108···It Hangs There

It hangs there
like an evil thing,
this curve of iron
that round some slave's neck
curled and snapped . . .
the slave long past,
his collar worn rib-thin,
rigid in rust
as if at last
its own rigor mortis
had set in.

P.S. The old iron slave collar from Jamaica hangs over my desk.

109···Passing the Blame

It was very near supper, and my instructions were clear, "No watermelon!"

Soon after, when I went out the front door, I discovered watermelon juice punctuated with seeds all over the stone steps. I summoned the young culprit.

"I didn't do it," he said flatly.

"You have to have," I replied, indicating the mess.

"No. Bea did it."

Now, Beatrice had been with us since before this character was born. At times I felt she was the mother and I the assistant mother. The idea of Beatrice sitting on the front steps eating watermelon and spitting seeds was ludicrous—particularly since she was inside preparing supper.

"Come with me," I said. "I think we'd better get this settled." In the bedroom I faced him: "Listen, Bud, God knows exactly what happened."

"Aw, Mom," the small voice interrupted, "Him doesn't know. Him's just guessing."

"Ned," I replied firmly. "He *saw*. Now let's get on our knees, and you tell Him you are sorry that you disobeyed and lied to cover it up."

Thinking about this, I had to conclude that we have become a generation of escape artists. It began, actually, in the Garden of Eden. Children go wrong—the parents are to blame; students erupt—the school has failed; prisoners riot—the prison system has failed; mass murders increase—society has failed. Adam was perhaps the only man who has not blamed his failure on his forebears or his genes. He blamed his wife.

Then I came across a confession from the old Episcopal Prayer Book:

I have sinned:
By my fault,
By my own fault,
By my own most grievous fault.

Perhaps we need to face up to the fact that reasons are not excuses. And while a person is not always responsible for what happens to him or her, each individual is responsible for how he or she reacts to circumstances. We are all ultimately responsible to God.

110 ···· The Bootblack and the Ph.D.

The small bootblack polished away with enthusiasm. He liked his work—turning a pair of scruffy leather shoes into a shining work of art.

He liked the men who called him by name, sat in his chair, and buried their noses in the morning newspaper.

He especially liked the little foreign man with the funny accent.

His friendly, "Today, how you are?" let him know this man really cared how he was. What the bootblack did not know was that the man with the funny accent was from Soviet Georgia and held three earned doctoral degrees. He just kept polishing away happily.

The day came when the unhappy Ph.D. could stand it no longer. Looking down at the bootblack working so cheerfully and enthusiastically on his shoes, and thinking on his own inner misery, he put down his paper.

"Why always you so happy?" he asked.

Surprised, the bootblack paused in his polishing, sat back on his heels, scratched his head thoughtfully for a moment, then said simply, "Jesus. He loves me. He died so God could forgive my badness. He makes me happy."

The newspaper snapped up around the face of the professor, and the bootblack went back to polishing his shoes.

But the brilliant University of Pennsylvania professor could not escape those simple words. They were what brought him eventually to the Savior.

Years later, my husband's college major was anthropology. His beloved and admired professor was the renowned Dr. Alexander Grigolia of the University of Pennsylvania, who found God through the simple testimony of a bootblack those many years before.

111···· Affluenza

"Lives based on having are less free than lives based either on doing or being."

—WILLIAM JAMES

Many of our coworkers had gathered for a time of inspiration, information, and refreshment.

Among them were Robert and Carol Cunville from India.

Sitting with us one night at dinner, Carol told me how their children had been begging to return to India.

"Here," they said, "there is too much."

···· ❧ ····

Bill and I were visiting with Nien Cheng, whose book *Life and Death in Shanghai* has caught the attention of literally thousands.

The small indomitable, aristocratic lady, looking at least twenty years younger than she should, made a startling statement.

"You know, I felt closer to God in solitary confinement in Shanghai than I do here in America.

"Here, there are so many distractions."

···· ❧ ····

Today, in the People's Republic of China the young people have become disillusioned and are growing frustrated and increasingly dissatisfied because they have so little. Little to work with, little to live for.

While here in America, we have what one writer referred to as "*affluenza.*" A feeling of guilt if one inherits a fortune, disillusionment on finding that "having too much is not enough."

We have produced a generation of dropouts, young people who, since the sixties, have disappeared into the drug culture, surfacing, incredibly, in the most unlikely parts of the earth.

"*Poverty,*" one has said, "*is a problem. But money is not the answer.*"

· · · · · ⚭ · · · · ·

> ". . . *we who strangely went astray*
>   *Lost in a bright*
>   *meridian night*
> *A darkness made of too much day.*"
> —RICHARD CRASHAW
> (1613–49)

112····Let Them Go

Let them go—
the things that have
accumulated thru the years.
If they be only things
then
let them go.
As barnacles
they but impede the ship
and slow
it down when it should go
full speed ahead.
Why dread
the disentangling?
Does the snake
regret the shedding
of its skin?
When the butterfly eludes
its chrysalis,
does regret
set in?

113 ···· "Why Me?"

Canon Bewes once told me about the time he invited Malcolm Muggeridge to speak at his church, All Souls, Langham Place, London.

All the local atheists showed up, relishing the unique opportunity. After the service there was a coffee, and Mr. Muggeridge answered questions. The general run of them went something like, "Why have you let us down?"

When Canon Bewes sensed time was up, he called for only one more question. Having dealt with that, Mr. Muggeridge noticed a boy in a wheelchair trying to say something. He stopped. "There is someone who wants to ask me a question. I will wait and answer it," he said.

Again the boy struggled to get the words out, but nothing came.

"Take your time," said Mr. Muggeridge reassuringly. "I want to hear what you have to ask, and I'll not leave till I hear it."

Then, as the boy's struggle continued to produce only agonized contortions, Mr. Muggeridge stepped down from the platform, walked to where the boy sat, put an arm around his shoulder, and said, "Just take it easy, son. It's all right. What is it you want to ask me? I want to hear, and I will just wait."

Finally, the boy blurted, "You say there is a God who loves us."

Mr. Muggeridge agreed.

"Then—why me?"

Silence filled the room. The boy was silent. The audience was silent. Mr. Muggeridge was silent. Finally, he asked, "If you were fit, would you have come to hear me tonight?"

The boy shook his head.

Again, Malcolm Muggeridge was silent. Then, "God has asked a hard thing of you," he said. "But remember He asked something even harder of Jesus Christ. He died for you. Maybe this was His way of making sure you'd hear of His love and come to put your faith in Him."

"Could be," said the boy.

114····Catfish

There is the story of the fishermen working in the North Sea off England bringing in their catch to the Billingsgate Wharf in the city of London. The fish, many of which had been caught days previously, were flabby. But one fisherman always had firm, fresh fish. However, he would not divulge his secret. After his death, his daughter passed it along. He always kept catfish in the well of the ship where the fish were stored. The catfish kept the other fish in such a constant state of irritation they did not have the opportunity to grow flabby.

· · · · · ～∞～ · · · · ·

"Many seem patient when they are not pricked."
—RICHARD ROLLE
Fourteenth Century

· · · · · ～∞～ · · · · ·

"Men strive for peace, but it is their enemies that give them strength, and I think if man no longer had enemies, he would have to invent them, for his strength only grows from struggle."
—ZACHARY VERNE
in The Lonesome Gods
by Louis L'Amour

· · · · · ～∞～ · · · · ·

"Hearty through hardship."
—GEORGE MACDONALD

115 ···· Dangerous Freedom

He had just emerged from existence under a regime that took a dim, even intolerant, view of Christianity. But now, viewing Christians who live not only in freedom but in relative comfort, this man was appalled. To him, these Christians seemed casual about their commitment, preoccupied with position and possessions, contaminated by the world. And he said so.

A few months later, he went back to visit the friend to whom he had spoken so bluntly when he first arrived. He asked if his friend remembered what he had said, the bitterness of his criticism. The friend remembered.

The man stood silent for a few moments, reflecting. The friend tensed for a second attack.

"I have come to apologize both for what I said and the way in which I said it," he said simply. "I was merely afraid. I did not know how dangerous freedom could be. It has been a year now. And I am worse than those I criticized."

Then he added a significant statement: "It is more difficult to live the Christian life under freedom than under repression."

116····He Fell on the Sidewalk

He fell on the sidewalk . . .
I saw him fall,
too drunk to walk
he could only crawl
to a scraggly tree
that grew near the street;
and with help of that tree
he got on his feet.
In my heart always,
God, help me see
he got on his feet
for—
      there was A Tree!

117···· "We Are Honored . . ."

He appeared at the door of the plane, saluted smartly, then made his way carefully down the steep steps. Stopping in front of the microphone, his rugged face haggard, yet calm, he said, *"We are honored to have served our country under difficult circumstances . . ."* America watched, moved by the sight of this man just released from years of captivity in North Vietnam, as he expressed his gratitude and ended unforgettably with, *"God bless America!"*

The man was Captain Jeremiah Denton. The date was February 11, 1973.

Those words, *"We are honored . . . ,"* have clung hauntingly to my mind down through the years. They were underscored in February, ten years later, when the film clip was again aired on national television accompanied in person by Jeremiah Denton, then a U.S. senator.

All this is a prelude to one thought: Is this how the believer will feel when he stands one day before God? Liberated from this earth and its struggles, will we say, "We are honored to have served . . . under difficult circumstances"?

God has entrusted to some of His servants the most difficult circumstances, and without explanations. We can go all the way back to Job, to Joseph in Egypt, Daniel in Babylon, the early martyrs, and on into the twentieth century where, we are told, there have been more martyrs in the Christian church than in the entire preceding two thousand years.

There is an apocryphal story of an early missionary whose first convert was tortured to death by indignant tribesmen. Years later, when the missionary died and went to Heaven, he met the convert and asked him how it felt to be tortured to death for Christ.

196

"You know," the man replied, looking puzzled. "I can't remember."

A young man recently released from an oppressive, atheistic regime was visiting a Christian family. "And what was it like, being persecuted for your faith?" his host asked.

"We thought it was the normal Christian life," was the surprising, yet candid, reply.

I think he was right. It is we Christians in the West who are living abnormally. Personally, I am grateful for the "abnormality." But if it doesn't last, we must not question, complain, or be bitter. Instead, let us accept each day as the Lord sends it, living obediently and faithfully, not fearing what may come, knowing that the glory ahead will obliterate the grim past, and praying we may be able to say to our Lord, "We are honored to have served . . . under difficult circumstances."

118 ···· *Something Better*

If God says "no" to something we want, it is because He has something better in store.

Years ago (1952), Bill and I were in London at the Howard Hotel on Norfolk Street on the Strand. While he was busy, two friends and I decided to go Foyles secondhand religious book department. Foyles is perhaps the largest secondhand bookstore in the world, and back then, its old used religious book department was an old-used-religious-book-lover's paradise.

Just as we headed out the door of the small Howard Hotel, I was met by a reporter requesting an interview.

Wishing the others "happy browsing," I returned to the lobby, inwardly frustrated and fretting, ordered tea for two, and waited for the questions.

"Where were you off to?"

"Foyles secondhand religious book department."

Eyebrows lifted inquiringly as the pencil poised in midair.

"Were you looking for—anything in particular?"

"As a matter of fact, I was. I was hoping to find an old unabridged copy of Foxe's *Book of Martyrs.*"

The fact duly noted, other questions answered to satisfaction, the tea was enjoyed, and after a few pleasantries, the reporter left.

When the piece came out in the paper, it mentioned the book I was looking for by name.

In a day or two I got a letter from a lady saying she had a two-volume set that had been in her family for over two hundred years. They had been slightly damaged in the blitz when the house next door suffered a direct hit by a bomb and was set on fire. The books, stored in a tin trunk in the basement, had received some resulting water damage. But if I was interested she

198

would let me have them—and she named, what I thought, was a very reasonable price.

I was interested. She got them to me, two huge volumes whose covers were damaged beyond repair, the pages yellowed with age and falling apart, a few with holes from age? mice? water damage?

It didn't really matter. I was holding over three hundred years, as it were, in my hands. (They were printed in 1631 and 1632, respectively.) The old, handmade paper, the priceless old etchings, the old lettering where "s" looked like "f."

I took them carefully to Foyles and asked if they could rebind them for me. "In leather," I added recklessly. An expert looked them over carefully and appreciatively. Yes, it could be done. And the damaged pages could be repaired—the holes not replaced, but repaired.

Later I picked up the two volumes, handmade, bound in brown leather. Foyles had done a beautiful job repairing and rebinding. They are among my most treasured books today.

119····Blinking

Blinking
back the tears,
I'm thinking,
may just clear
the heart for sight;
as windshield wipers
help us on
a stormy, windswept
night.

120···Of Jellyfish and Such

I could see the blond head of "Big Daddy," England's most famous wrestler. He was taking his daily constitutional in the deep, choppy waters of the Mediterranean when suddenly I heard him shout to his daughter, "Jan! Jan! A jellyfish just got me. Help!"

Rolling over in the water, I watched to see how tiny Jan could help her enormous daddy.

"He got me again!" his voice boomed.

Suddenly I was struck. It was as if my right arm touched a high-voltage wire. Spinning violently, my leg caught in a viselike cramp, I glimpsed the tiny blue jellyfish swimming away. Grateful for the safety rope beside me, I hung on, weak with shock and the incredible stinging, my right calf painfully knotted. It seemed an eternity before I was able to make it back the short distance to the beach, petrified that there might be a second close encounter of the first kind. It wasn't long before ugly welts rose around my right forearm and a livid red line crossed my back. By dinner time the pain had subsided to a bone-deep ache; the swelling lasted six weeks; the scars will last my lifetime.

Later, as "Big Daddy" and I compared stings, he inquired solicitously, "I hope you won't let this keep you from going into the water, will you?" His voice was both compassionate and concerned, and his granite face, with its blue eyes, was friendly and kind. I hadn't the heart to tell him I'd lost all taste for the sea, all trust of its "critters."

But two painful days later, assured by the beachboys and bathers that the sea was clear, I ventured another swim. Suddenly a familiar voice boomed, "Good for you! Didn't let that jellyfish put you off, did you?"

It was "Big Daddy" out for his hourly workout in the deep water, shouting encouragement to this one timid swimmer. "Good girl!" he responded to my wave. "Keep it up!" Here was a professional athlete, a giant of a man, an experienced swimmer, looking out for one of the poorest, least enthusiastic swimmers in the sea.

Life is a lot like the sea: full of unseen hazards and venomous creatures that attack without warning. I kept thinking of baby Christians who, after that first painful encounter, lose heart. Hurting and fearful, they call it quits unless some more experienced, stronger Christian offers a word of sympathetic advice, a shout of encouragement, and a note of praise.

Long after I'd forgotten the jellyfish attack and its painful aftermath, I remembered those words, "You won't let it keep you from going into the water, will you?" And later, "Good for you! Keep it up!"

Has anybody around you been stung lately?

121 ···· Why Are You Praying?

There are times, I have found, when praying is not enough. God says, as it were, "Why are you praying? Do something!"

Moses, hotly pursued by Pharaoh, cried out to God, who replied, *"Wherefore criest thou unto me? speak unto the children of Israel, that they go forward"* (EXODUS 14:15).

After Israel's ignominious defeat at Ai, the desperate Joshua prostrated himself in prayer before the Lord, only to hear Him say, "Wherefore liest thou thus upon thy face? Israel hath sinned" (JOSHUA 7:10–11).

"The polite part of speaking with God is to be still long enough to listen," Edward Gloeggler has suggested.

If our hearts are listening as we pray, we will from time to time, hear "Why are you praying? Do something!" And we will know what it is that we must do. A wrong to put right, a sin to confess, a letter to write, a friend to visit, or perhaps a child to be rocked and read to.

C. S. Lewis suggests in *Letters to Malcom* that as we pray, Christ stands beside us changing us. *"This may send a man,"* he wrote, *"from his prayers to help his wife in the kitchen or to his desk to write a needed letter."* And again, *"I am often, I believe, praying for others when I should be doing things for them. It is so much easier to pray for a boor than to go and see him."*

122···Someone's Listening

Arthur Schnabel defined *great music* as *"music that is composed better than it can be played."* I think the same can be said of Christianity. Only One has played the score perfectly, and He was the Composer. Some people have done magnificently. Others seem to forget the score halfway through, while still others never get past the practice stage. Most players are just average.

But the score, as God wrote it, and as our Lord Himself lived it, is the most beautiful the world has ever heard.

Beethoven wrote some of his greatest music after he became deaf. Though he never heard it, he composed music *"better than it can be played."*

There was another musician in a land where for years "God's music" was not allowed to be played. Daily he took out his score of Handel's *Messiah* and placed it on the dining room table. Then, on the table, his fingers silently and diligently played through the entire score. "He was making music," commented a friend, "'that only God could hear.'"

Anything worth doing well takes practice. I listen to great pianists, watch the Olympic athletes, hear about surgeons who perform incredible operations. And then I think of the hours of daily practice over the years that brought them to that place. It is easy to become casual in a land where Christianity is accepted.

If there are any regrets in Heaven, perhaps they will be that given such beautiful music to play—music *"composed better than it can be played"*—most of us have practiced so casually, so little.

123 ··· Someone Has to Pay

Lunch finished, I picked up my check and, after a passing glance, did a double take.

I had lunched alone, without indulging in dessert. There were three desserts on my bill.

Summoning my little waitress, I pointed out the error.

"Oh, I know," she shrugged offhandedly, "but the people before you left without paying, and I had to put it on somebody's bill."

Needless to say, I paid my bill—minus the three desserts.

124 ··· I Awoke to a World

I awoke to a world
of whitening wonder:
all the bareness of
winter landscape under
soft white snow
fallen—
    and still falling—
as the dusk falls.
The mountains 'round
are whited out—
and still it falls,
leaving only the nearer woods
etched stark against
the white about.
The only color I can see
—a red bird in a whitened tree;
The only sound
in a world gone still:
a towhee on my windowsill.

125 ··· "It's Enough"

Elijah, the prophet of God, has just had a showdown with the priests of Baal, then wiped them out. The brook Kishon ran red before the day was done.

Now Baal worship was as sick and depraved and diabolical as any idol worship could be. (In case you feel Elijah was too hard on them, read a description of Baal worship as found in James Michener's *The Source*.)

And King Ahab told his wife, Queen Jezebel—whose special proteges the priests were.

It was one thing to stand up to King Ahab, the 450 prophets of Baal, and the 400 prophets of the groves who ate at Jezebel's table. It was quite another to stand up to Jezebel.

Also Elijah was emotionally drained from the preceding day's events, and physically exhausted from having run before Ahab's chariot the twenty miles to the entrance of Jezreel.

Then from Jezreel to Beersheba, a distance of around one hundred miles as the crow flies. And Elijah was flying. He left his faithful servant at Beersheba and went another day's journey into the wilderness, collapsed under a juniper tree, and prayed, *"It is enough; now, O Lord, take away my life."*

Not "it is finished" but *"it is enough."*

The Lord knew what His servant needed. Sleep and nourishment. And God provided just that (see I Kings 19).

"How many problems," someone has said, *"are solved by a good night's sleep."*

· · · · · ◦⟋⟍◦ · · · · ·

I found myself chuckling on a sunny beach one winter.

I had saved a whole list of problems to work out in the quiet of our winter vacation. And there in the warm sun, with the blue-green waters of the Caribbean gently advancing and retreating on the sand beside me, I could not remember a single one.

But I was not Elijah, nor had I gone through what he had gone through—nor had Jezebel threatened to do *"so to me and more also"* as Elijah had done to her pet prophets.

But someone realizing this might be feeling you had just about had it—desertion, rejection, illness, bills for which there is no money, death, the deep concern of someone dearly loved who is in deep trouble or is hurting unbelievably.

And like Elijah, we're prone to pray, "Lord, it is enough."

· · · · · ⤳⤲ · · · · ·

Jesus had faced the forces of hell and fought them to a standstill. It was not just the outcome of one day's incredible work, but the culmination of thirty-three years of life on earth; thirty as carpenter and three of public teaching, healing, and continual confrontations with the religious leaders of His day. And the cross lay just ahead.

Someone pointed out that Jesus did not feed all the hungry, heal all the sick, cure all the cripples, or raise all the dead. Yet when He came to the end of His life's work just before His crucifixion, He said, *"I have finished the work which thou gavest me to do"* (JOHN 17:4).

How often in my life I have said, "It's enough!"

But we each have our "Plimsoll mark" (that line around ocean tankers to indicate when the load has reached its maximum capacity). He who made us knows just how much we can take. He never overloads us. But *"neither has He promised strength for uncommanded tasks."*

208

I want Him to so order my life that when the end comes I can say, "I have finished the work which thou gavest me to do."

I do not want to feel compelled to say, "It is enough" before I can honestly say, with His help, "It is finished."

126 ··· Tonight the Lights Went Out

Tonight
the lights went out,
(aftermath of a sudden storm)
trapped in dark
I groped about
to light the candles
and a fire
to keep me warm;
wondering how
men manage, who
have no fire, no candlelight
to company them some
stormy night.

127···He Watched a Christian Die

Someone has said, *"If there had not been a Stephen, there might never have been a Paul."*

• • • • • ⤫ • • • • •

A tribal war was raging in Uganda.

The soldiers led a line of prisoners to a bridge over a crocodile-infested river where they could shoot them and dump their bodies into the water for the crocodiles to dispose of.

Among the prisoners that day was a young Christian. When his turn came to be shot, he asked permission to say a word first.

"Make it quick," his captors ordered.

The young man looked at them calmly, without fear.

"I am a Christian," he said.

"I am not angry with you, for the same Jesus Whom I shall see in a few moments died for you as well. I forgive you. May you accept His forgiveness also."

They shot him.

Turning to the next in line, they recognized a man from another tribe.

"What are you doing here?" they demanded. "We are not at war." And he was abruptly dismissed.

• • • • • ⤫ • • • • •

But that young man was never the same again. He spent the rest of his life sharing his new discovery of the risen, transforming Savior.

He had watched a Christian die.

128···Where Are You?

We were standing in front of Buckingham Palace with crowds of tourists waiting for the changing of the guard. An American couple behind me were trying to decide just where they were. Their map was open as far as the packed crowd would allow.

"I wonder," said the man, "if this building behind us could happen to be Buckingham Palace."

No authority myself, I knew at least that much. Asking to see their map, I hastily showed them where they were and tried to point out a few more visible places of interest.

So we missed seeing the Duchess of Kent being driven past. The crowd was too busy with the changing of the guard to notice her either.

A few seconds later, the Queen herself was driven past, again unnoticed by the crowd preoccupied with the changing of the guard. It was our friend Ruth King, who misses nothing, who told us what we had missed while our noses were buried in guide maps and our eyes focused on the changing of the guard.

Tourists are a breed to themselves. They rush through a country, glancing at what they are supposed to see, often unsure of what they are seeing, and occasionally so preoccupied with the obvious that they miss what is really important.

Our next stop was Westminster Abbey. While my sister, Rosa, dashed madly through nine hundred years of English history, I sat on a concrete post outside to catch up on my journal. An American couple were walking by with their young son, who asked his parents, "Do you suppose this is the Wax Works?" I have heard of people having an identity crisis—but this had to be a "location crisis"—a not uncommon problem among tourists.

On my trip around the world in 1980, which began with the pilgrimage to our family home and birthplace in the People's Republic of China, it was a common thing to wake up wondering, "Where am I?" Every few days we would find ourselves in a different room, a different city, and even a different country.

· · · · · ⟨ornament⟩ · · · · ·

It was opening night of the World Missions Conference in Montreat. Daddy, who had just completed his year as moderator of the Southern Presbyterian Church, had been asked to open the conference with prayer. Before he did so, he said, "Before I pray I have a few words to say . . . Now in this place there are two groups of people. There are those who know that they are saved and love the Lord Jesus Christ, and there are those here who as yet may not know Christ. My hope is that before you leave this place you will come to know Him as your personal Lord and Savior. The Lord said, 'Behold, I stand at the door, and knock: if any man hear My voice, and open the door, I will come in to him, and will sup with him, and he with Me.'"

That was all.

Early the next morning he was in the actual presence of the Lord he loved and served so faithfully and joyously.

Do you know where you are today? Have you been born into God's family through faith in His Son our Savior? Or are you still outside?

Many of Paul's epistles begin: "*Paul to the brethren in Christ which are at* [some city]." Someone has suggested that "*in Christ*" was their home address while "*at Colosse*" or some other city was their business address. Wherever we may travel in this world, we can be secure in knowing that our home address is "*in Christ*," wherever our business address may be.

Where are you?

129 ··· Autographed by the Author

The heavy, flat package was from Ottawa, Ontario, in Canada.

Quickly tearing off the wrappings, I discovered with delight a portfolio by the famous photographer, Yousuf Karsh. Each page held one of his remarkable photographs, and on the back, the photographer's comment on the subject and the sitting.

Wondering who had sent the book, I turned to the front and to my amazement discovered an inscription to Bill from the author, Yousuf Karsh.

As I gathered the torn wrappings, I noted the customs sticker. "Autographed by the author" is what was written to describe the value of the contents.

I recently reread an essay I had written at the age of fourteen when I was a sophomore at the Pyengyang Foreign School in what is now Pyong Yang, North Korea. It is titled "The Name of Jesus," and it closes by quoting Revelation 3:12 ". . . *and I will write upon him My new name.*"

The essay concluded: "If His present name is so wonderful, what will His new name be which He has promised to write upon us if we overcome in this world?"

Some of us, however, feel more overcome than that we are overcomers. And we find comfort in Dr. Way's translation of Philippians 2:13: "Ye . . . *have not to do it in your own unaided strength; it is God who is all the while supplying the impulse, giving you the power to resolve, the strength to perform the execution of his good pleasure.*"

Our ultimate value will be that we were not only created, compiled and, as it were, written by the author. Our true value will rest in the fact that we have been autographed by the Author.

130 ··· "Pure Joy"

"God is preparing His heroes. And when the opportunity comes, He can fit them into their places in a moment. And the world will wonder where they came from."

—A. B. SIMPSON

· · · · · ⬳⬳⬳ · · · · ·

In the summer of 1978 we were in Stockholm, Sweden.

I had been asked to address a group of ladies.

Two interpreters came to my rescue: one to interpret what I would be saying to the ladies, the other to interpret to me all that was being said in Swedish. Both happened to be stalwarts in the Salvation Army.

The one sitting beside me telling me what was going on was Gunvar Paulson.

Do you recall reading in the press during the summer of 1977 how a group of insurgents had attacked the Salvation Army mission station in Rhodesia, killing two of the women missionaries and leaving a third for dead? This was the third. Her left arm had been badly shot up, and although she had undergone repeated surgeries, she had only limited use of it.

Impulsively I leaned over and whispered how honored I was to be sitting beside her as I had never had to suffer for my Lord the way she had.

"Believe me," she replied simply, with a smile. "It was a joy."

Then, perhaps noticing the wonder on my face, she added,

"You know, I never had to suffer for my Lord before this happened. And in spite of the horrors going on all around me at the time, there was such a sense of the presence of the Lord Jesus Himself that it was pure joy."

131 ···· Faith Versus Reason

Picasso was once quoted as *"praying for strength to transcend the limits his reason was trying to impose on him."*

His paintings show that he succeeded admirably.

However, there are limits imposed by reason other than one's imagination. I am thinking of that vital area of faith, *"without which it is impossible to please God."*

An old writer says,

"Faith and reason can be compared to two travelers: Faith is like a man in full health, who can walk his 20 or 30 miles at a time without suffering. Reason is like a child, who can only with difficulty accomplish 3 or 4 miles.

"Well," says this old writer, *"on a given day Reason says to Faith, 'O good Faith, let me walk with you.'*

"Faith replies, 'O Reason, you can never walk with me.'

"However, to try their paces, they set out together but they soon find it hard to keep company. When they come to a deep river, Reason says, 'I can never ford this.' But Faith wades through singing.

"When they reach a lofty mountain, there is the same exclamation of despair, and in such cases, Faith, in order not to leave Reason behind, is obliged to carry him on his shoulder."

And, adds the writer,

"Oh, what a luggage is Reason to Faith!"

Blaise Pascal wrote in The Pensées, *"The last step that reason takes is to recognize that there is an infinity of things beyond it."*

216

He also says, "*A unit joined to infinity adds nothing to it, any more than one foot added to infinite length. The finite is annihilated in the presence of infinity and becomes pure zero. So is our intellect before God.*"

And, "*The heart feels God, not the reason. This is what constitutes faith. God experienced by the heart, not by the reason.*"

And, "*The heart has its reasons of which the reason knows nothing.*"

132 ··· "There's Robby!"

Mr. Armistead's younger son Humphrey, who was twelve at the time of this story, grew up to become pastor of the Friendship Presbyterian Church between Montreat and Black Mountain, North Carolina. In Montreat, after his death, his lovely widow, Lucille, told me this story in 1967. I wrote it down in a notebook. But to make sure I had it accurately and also to ask permission to include it in this book, I wrote to Lucille Armistead, who is living in Florida.

Her gracious reply, on her return from celebrating her eighty-ninth birthday with her son, said, *"I am so glad to send you the story, and I'm happy that you will use it."*

I checked her account with my twenty-one-year-old notes. They were, except for small, unimportant details, identical.

· · · · · ∽⌒⌒⌒∾ · · · · ·

The room was quiet and semidarkened. The elderly lady lying against the pillows listened as her son, Robert, talked of the family, her friends, and other things of interest to her.

She looked forward to his daily visits. Madison, where he lived, was not far from Nashville, and Robert spent as much time as he could with his mother, knowing, as ill as she was, each visit might be his last. As he talked, his eyes took in every detail of her loved face, every line—and there were more lines than curves now—the white hair, the tired, still loving eyes. When time came to leave, he kissed her gently on her forehead, assuring her he would be back the next day.

Arriving back at his home in Madison, he found Robin, his seventeen-year-old, was ill with a strange fever.

218

The next few days his time was completely taken up between his son and his mother.

He did not tell his mother of Robin's illness. He was her oldest grandson—the pride and joy of her life.

Then, suddenly, Robin was gone. His death shocked the whole community as well as his family. The whole thing had happened so quickly. And seventeen is too young to die.

As soon as the funeral was over, Mr. Armistead hurried to his mother's bedside, praying nothing in his manner would betray the fact he had just buried his firstborn. It would be more than his mother could take in her condition.

The doctor was in the room as he entered. His mother was lying with her eyes closed.

"She is in a coma," the doctor said gently. He knew something of the strain this man had been under, his faithful visits to his mother, the death of his son, the funeral from which he had just come . . .

The doctor put his hand on Mr. Armistead's shoulder in wordless sympathy.

"Just sit beside her," he said, "she might come to . . ." And he left them together.

Mr. Armistead's heart was heavy as he sat in the gathering twilight.

He lit the lamp on the bedside table, and the shadows receded.

Soon she opened her eyes, and smiling in recognition, she put her hand on her son's knee.

"Bob . . . ," she said his name lovingly—and drifted into a coma again.

Quietly Mr. Armistead sat on, his hand over hers, his eyes never leaving her face. After awhile there was a slight movement on the pillow.

His mother's eyes were open and there was a far-off look in them, as if she were seeing beyond the room. A look of wonder passed over her face.

"I see Jesus," she exclaimed, adding, "why there's Father . . . and there's Mother . . ."

And then,

"And there's Robby! I didn't know Robby had died . . ."
Her hand patted her son's knee gently.
"Poor Bob . . . ," she said softly, and was gone.

"Heaven: where questions and answers become one."
— ELIE WIESEL

$$\cdots\cdots\;\infty\;\cdots\cdots$$

"And when the storm is passed, the brightness for which He is preparing us will shine out unclouded, and it will be Himself."
— MOTHER GRAHAM
to her companion, Rose Adams,
on the death of Rose's husband

$$\cdots\cdots\;\infty\;\cdots\cdots$$

" 'Who plucked that flower?' asked the gardner.
'The Master,' was the reply. And the gardner held his peace."
— JOHN BUNYAN

$$\cdots\cdots\;\infty\;\cdots\cdots$$

"As the years passed she was disturbed, almost alarmed, by the growing peace and serenity of her days. Surely it was wrong to be so happy. Then abruptly she knew it was not wrong. This was the ending of her days on earth, the dawn of her heavenly days, and it had been given to her to feel the sun on her face."
— MISS MONTAGUE
in The Dean's Watch
by Elizabeth A. Goudge